DK Pocket Genius

SPACE

FACTS AT YOUR FINGERTIPS

DK DELHI
Project editor Bharti Bedi
Senior editor Kingshuk Ghoshal
Senior art editor Rajnish Kashyap
Art editors Isha Nagar, Mahipal Singh
Assistant editor Priyanka Kharbanda
Assistant art editor Aanchal Singal
DTP designers Sachin Singh, Vishal Bhatia
Picture researcher Sumedha Chopra

DK LONDON
Senior editor Rob Houston
Senior art editor Philip Letsu
US editor Margaret Parrish
Jacket editor Manisha Majithia
Jacket designer Laura Brim
Jacket manager Amanda Lunn
Production editor Rebekah Parsons-King
Production controller Mary Slater
Publisher Andrew Macintyre
Associate publishing director Liz Wheeler
Art director Phil Ormerod
Publishing director Jonathan Metcalf
Consultant Dr. Jacqueline Mitton

TALL TREE LTD.
Editors Rob Colson, Joe Fullman, Jon Richards
Art editor Ed Simkins

First American Edition, 2012
This edition published in the United States in 2016 by DK
Publishing, 1450 Broadway, Suite 801, New York, NY 10018

A catalog record for this book
is available from the Library of Congress.
ISBN: 978-1-4654-4593-3

DK books are available at special discounts when purchased in
bulk for sales promotions, premiums, fund-raising, or educational
use. For details, contact: DK Publishing Special Markets,
1450 Broadway, Suite 801, New York, NY 10018
SpecialSales@dk.com

Printed and bound in China

A WORLD OF IDEAS:
SEE ALL THERE IS TO KNOW

www.dk.com

CONTENTS

4 What is out there?
6 The scale of the universe
8 The Big Bang
10 What is the universe made of?
12 The electromagnetic spectrum
14 Mapping the night sky
16 The northern sky
18 The southern sky

22 STUDYING SPACE
24 How telescopes work
26 Ground-based telescopes
30 Space telescopes

34 THE SOLAR SYSTEM
36 The Sun's family
38 The rocky planets
40 The giant planets
44 Planetary features
56 The Moon
58 Moons
66 Dwarf planets
68 Asteroids
70 Comets
72 Meteorites

74 STARS AND NEBULAE
76 Life cycle of a star
78 Stars
82 Star clusters
86 Exoplanets
88 Nebulae

98 GALAXIES
100 What is a galaxy?
102 Galaxies

116 EXPLORING SPACE
118 Types of spacecraft
120 Rockets
124 Spacecraft
138 Manned missions
142 Space stations

146 Timeline of space exploration
148 Amazing facts
150 Glossary
152 Index
155 Acknowledgments

Scales and sizes
This book contains profiles of planets, moons, telescopes, and spacecraft next to scale drawings to show how big they are.

7,926 miles (12,756 km)
Earth

2,160 miles (3,476 km)
Moon

231 ft (70 m)
Boeing 747

6 ft (1.8 m)
Human

Locators
Earth locator maps show surface features, locations of telescopes, or impact sites of meteorites. Moon locators show lunar features.

Other locator maps show the location of a star, galaxy, or nebula within a constellation.

What is out there?

The stars that dot the night sky are only a few of the billions of stars in the universe. Stars are born inside dense clouds of gas and dust called nebulae, and form groups known as galaxies. Balls of ice, rock, or gas known as planets move around, or orbit, many stars. Planet Earth orbits a star called the Sun and is the only place in the universe known to support life.

What is a galaxy?

Every star is part of a group called a galaxy. Galaxies range in size from dwarf ones made up of around 10 million stars to giant galaxies, which can have more than 1 trillion stars. Galaxies can have different shapes—the Southern Pinwheel Galaxy, for example, looks like a spiral with long, curved arms.

What is a star?

Stars may look like specks of light in the night sky, but they are actually huge balls of hot gas—mainly hydrogen and helium. The Sun is a star but looks much larger than the other stars because it is a lot closer to Earth.

Interstellar clouds

Space is not as empty as it seems. Gas and particles of dust grains float in interstellar space (the regions between stars). In some places, the gas and dust form dense clouds called nebulae. The Horsehead nebula appears as a dark shape because it blocks light from the stars behind it.

Planets and moons

A planet is a body large enough to be shaped into a ball by its own gravity. Planets orbit stars. Smaller bodies called moons orbit some planets. Eight planets orbit the Sun, including Mars, the "red planet." It is the fourth planet from the Sun and has two small moons.

Other bodies

The group of bodies orbiting the Sun includes many small chunks of rock and ice, such as dwarf planets, asteroids, and comets. Most circle the Sun in regions called belts, including the Asteroid Belt between Mars and Jupiter, and the Kuiper Belt beyond the outermost planet.

The scale of the universe

The Sun is the closest star to Earth and lies about 93 million miles (150 million km) away. The next nearest star is thousands of times farther, while the farthest galaxies are billions of times more distant yet. Scientists may never be able to calculate how big the universe really is.

Our place in space

Earth forms part of the solar system, which lies in one of the arms of the Milky Way galaxy. The galaxy forms part of a cluster of galaxies, which is just one of many galaxy clusters scattered across the universe.

Distances in the universe

The distances in space are so great that special units called light-years are used to measure them. A light-year is the distance light travels in a year—about 5.9 trillion miles (9.46 trillion km).

Earth has a diameter of 7,926 miles (12,756 km).

Earth is the third planet in the **solar system**. Scientists believe the edge of the solar system is about 6 trillion miles (10 trillion km) away from Earth.

Distance (light-years)

1	10	100	1000	10,000

Sun (0.000016 light-years)

Edge of solar system (1 light-year)

Proxima Centauri (4 light-years)

Center of Milky Way (26,000 light-years)

Redshift

The universe is expanding. We know this because all galaxy clusters are moving apart. Scientists measure a galaxy's speed by studying its light. The light waves from a galaxy speeding away from Earth are stretched out making them longer and redder. This is called redshift.

Light from galaxy moving away from observer looks redder

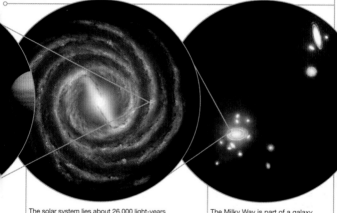

The solar system lies about 26,000 light-years from the center of the **Milky Way**, in one of the galaxy's spiral arms, as shown in this artist's impression (drawing based on scientific data).

The Milky Way is part of a galaxy cluster called the **Local Group**, which spans a region about 10 million light-years across.

100,000	1 million	10 million	100 million	1 billion	10 billion

Andromeda Galaxy
(2.6 million light-years)

Virgo galaxy cluster
(53.8 million light-years)

Edge of the known
universe (13.8 billion
light-years)

The Big Bang

Around 13.8 billion years ago, the universe was born in a colossal explosion known as the Big Bang, which produced matter and energy. The universe formed in a tiny fraction of a second. At this point, it was very dense and incredibly hot. It grew and cooled, eventually forming stars and galaxies.

The **expansion of the universe** that began with the Big Bang continues today. In fact, the universe is expanding more and more quickly. Scientists have found that it has been speeding up for 5 billion years but are not sure what will happen in the future.

Evolution of the universe

Scientists are not sure what triggered the Big Bang. They can, however, trace the history of the universe to a fraction of a second after the Big Bang. The energy released at this point formed the particles that became the building blocks of stars, planets, and galaxies.

The **Big Bang** released the hot, new universe in all directions.

Scientists can detect the energy given off by the early universe, around 400,000 years after the Big Bang. This energy is known as the cosmic microwave background radiation, and its pattern is shown here in blue and green.

The **first atoms** formed about 400,000 years after the Big Bang. They were atoms of the gases hydrogen and helium.

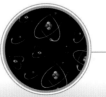

The **first stars** formed around 200 million years after the Big Bang when gravity pulled clouds of hydrogen and helium into dense clumps.

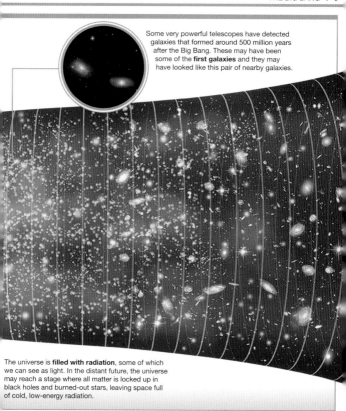

Some very powerful telescopes have detected galaxies that formed around 500 million years after the Big Bang. These may have been some of the **first galaxies** and they may have looked like this pair of nearby galaxies.

The universe is **filled with radiation**, some of which we can see as light. In the distant future, the universe may reach a stage where all matter is locked up in black holes and burned-out stars, leaving space full of cold, low-energy radiation.

What is the universe made of?

The universe contains matter and energy. Stars and galaxies are examples of matter that can be seen, but galaxies also contain invisible "dark matter." It does not give off light or heat and so is hard to find. It can, however, be detected by the effects of its gravity on visible objects.

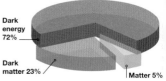

Dark energy 72%

Dark matter 23%

Matter 5%

Composition

Visible matter makes up only 5 percent of the entire universe, while the invisible dark matter has a much larger share. Greater still is a mysterious force called dark energy, which is causing the universe to expand.

Matter

Matter is anything that has mass and is affected by gravity. All matter is made up of particles called atoms, which in turn are made of smaller particles. Atoms are far too small to be seen. There are four main states of matter—solid, liquid, gas, and plasma—depending on how closely the atoms are packed.

Neutron lies at the center, or nucleus, of an atom

Proton also lies in the nucleus

Helium atom contains 2 protons, 2 neutrons, and 2 electrons

Electron orbits around the nucleus

Dark matter

Dark matter is scattered across the universe. Since it is invisible, the only clue to its existence comes from watching visible matter. Some large clusters of galaxies, such as Abell 901/902, seem to have a gravitational pull far stronger than expected. Scientists think the extra gravity is caused by dark matter.

STUDYING DARK MATTER

The **Large Hadron Collider** at the European organization for Nuclear Research (CERN) at Geneva is a colossal underground machine. Scientists use it to recreate the conditions similar to just after the Big Bang, which may help them to understand how dark matter forms.

 A **solid**, such as these gold bars, has a fixed shape.

 Liquid matter, such as oil, has no fixed shape unless held in a container.

Gas particles, such as bromine vapor, move around freely. A gas has no fixed shape.

 Plasma forms when gas is heated until its atoms break apart. Plasma in this ball was made by running electricity through gas.

The electromagnetic spectrum

Light waves, radio waves, and X-rays are all forms of energy-carrying waves called electromagnetic (EM) radiation. Stars, galaxies, and other objects in space give off the entire range of EM radiation. This range, from low to high energy, is called the EM spectrum.

Waves of energy

EM waves travel at the speed of light—about 186,000 miles (300,000 km) per second—but carry different amounts of energy depending on the length of their waves. Wavelength is the distance from the top of one wave to the top of the next. Seen here is the Crab Nebula in different wavelengths. False colors show the invisible radiation.

Radio waves have wavelengths several yards long, but less energy than other forms of radiation.

Infrared radiation, or heat, from hot gas and dust is seen in red, while that from speeding electrons appears blue.

Radio waves
    Microwaves
        Infrared

Wavelengths between radio and infrared

Visible light is the radiation that we can see with our eyes. Gas and electrons in the Crab Nebula both produce visible light. Light ranges from long-wavelength red light to short-wavelength violet.

Gamma rays have the shortest wavelengths and the most energy. A spinning neutron star (see p.77) at the nebula's center produces these gamma rays.

Ultraviolet rays have shorter wavelengths than visible light. The incredibly hot central region of the nebula gives off these waves.

X-rays are high-energy waves released by very hot material. Seen here are superhot particles at the nebula's center, which are giving off X-rays.

Visible light

Ultraviolet

X-rays

Gamma rays

Mapping the night sky

The night sky is filled with stars. To find a way around these scattered points of light, it is useful to see the night sky in the same way that ancient astronomers saw it—as a giant sphere surrounding Earth. These astronomers also saw patterns of stars in the night sky, which they called constellations.

North celestial pole lies above Earth's North Pole

Mars

The celestial sphere

People find objects on Earth's surface using an imaginary grid. The grid has a line called the equator dividing the planet into two halves. Latitude lines run round Earth either side of the equator, while longitude lines run from pole to pole. In the same way, astronomers imagine lines on the celestial sphere. It has a celestial north and south pole, and a celestial equator. Grid lines running from pole to pole are called lines of right ascension (RA), while lines running either side of the celestial equator are lines of declination. Each object in Earth's sky can be located using the points where these lines meet. The celestial sphere helps astronomers track the movements of objects in the night sky as Earth spins.

Sun

Mercury

Venus

The Sun is not fixed on the celestial sphere but seems to move around it along a path called the **ecliptic**

Declination is the celestial sphere's equivalent of latitude and is measured in degrees and minutes

Right ascension is the celestial sphere's equivalent of longitude and is measured in hours and minutes

Earth's **equator**

Celestial equator lies above Earth's equator

Jupiter

Saturn

Moon

The Moon and planets seem to move within a narrow band on either side of the ecliptic. The constellations seen in this band form the **Zodiac**.

South celestial pole lies above Earth's South Pole

Starhopping

Astronomers and amateur sky watchers find their way around the night sky by starhopping. First they spot a star or star pattern that is easy to recognize. Then they trace an imaginary line to a nearby star and hop to that, repeating the process until the target star is in sight.

The two bright stars at the end of Ursa Major's "Big Dipper," Dubhe and Merak, point the way to Polaris, or the North star, at the top.

The three bright stars in Orion's belt point towards the giant red star Aldebaran in Taurus.

The northern sky

The stars we see in the night sky change depending on our latitude, the time of night, and the time of the year. As Earth orbits the Sun, different parts of the celestial sphere appear above us, which means that we see a changing sequence of constellations over a year. Astronomers use the constellations to identify the positions of objects in the sky.

Northern constellations

The stars and constellations of the northern half of the celestial sphere are shown on the sky map (opposite) as if lying on a flat surface. At the center of the map lies the star Polaris, which appears to remain directly over Earth's North Pole.

Delphinus
Kite-shaped Delphinus lies near the constellation Cygnus and represents a dolphin jumping out of water.

Creating constellations

Ancient Babylonian and Greek astronomers traced figures of gods and animals from their myths and legends in the skies, creating constellations. Modern astronomers recognize 88 constellations.

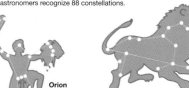

Orion
In Greek myth, Orion was a mighty hunter. The row of three bright stars forms Orion's belt, a "skymark" that is easy to locate.

Leo
The pattern of the stars look like the outline of a crouching lion. Six stars make up the lion's head and chest and are known as the Sickle.

Taurus
This represents the head and upper body of a mythical bull. The stars Beta Tauri and Zeta Tauri lie at the tips of the bull's horns.

The **Milky Way** is the faint band of starlight that circles the celestial sphere

Ecliptic

SAGITTARIUS

SCORPIUS

SERPENS CAUDA

SCUTUM

CAPRICORNUS

LIBRA

OPHIUCHUS

AQUILA

AQUARIUS

PISCES AUSTRINUS

SERPENS CAPUT

SAGITTA

VULPECULA

DELPHINUS

EQUULEUS

HERCULES

LYRA

CYGNUS

PEGASUS

CORONA BOREALIS

BOÖTES

DRACO

CEPHEUS

CETUS

VIRGO

HYDRA

URSA MINOR

CASSIOPEIA

PISCES

CORVUS

COMA BERENICES

CANES VENATICI

Polaris

CAMELOPARDALIS

ANDROMEDA

PERSEUS

TRIANGULUM

ARIES

CRATER

SEXTANS

LEO MINOR

URSA MAJOR

LEO

LYNX

AURIGA

TAURUS

ERIDANUS

HYDRA

CANCER

GEMINI

ORION

CANIS MINOR

MONOCEROS

LEPUS

CANIS MAJOR

Celestial equator

Northern half of celestial sphere

The southern sky

The stars and constellations of the southern half of the celestial sphere are shown on this sky map as if lying on a flat surface. The stars around the edge of the map can be seen from both the northern and southern hemispheres. Earth's South Pole lines up with the center of this map.

The Zodiac

Over a year, the Sun appears to travel through a band of constellations around the sky called the Zodiac. These constellations are: Aries, Taurus, Gemini, Cancer, Leo, Virgo, Libra, Scorpio, Sagittarius, Capricorn, Aquarius, and Pisces.

Aquarius
In Greek mythology, Aquarius was a shepherd who became a waiter to the Olympian Gods. This constellation contains the Helix Nebula (see pp.92–93).

Sagittarius
Sagittarius was a centaur in Greek mythology—a half-human, half-horse creature. Deep-space objects in this constellation include the Lagoon Nebula (see p.88).

Scorpius
This depicts the scorpion that, in Greek mythology, killed the hunter Orion with its sting. The constellation Scorpius is in the direction of the center of our galaxy, the Milky Way.

Pisces
The constellation Pisces represents two mythical fish. A distinctive ring of seven stars, known as the Circlet, makes up the body of one of the creatures.

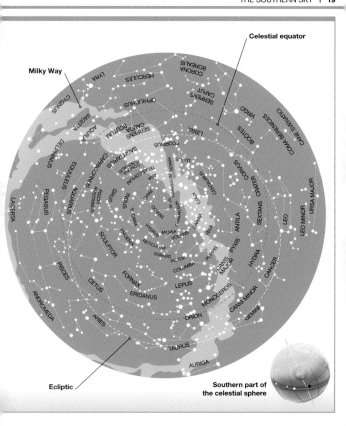

Celestial equator

Milky Way

Ecliptic

Southern part of
the celestial sphere

THE MILKY WAY
Our galaxy, which we call the Milky Way, is disk-shaped. Our solar system is located within the disk, which means that we see the combined light of its billions of stars as a hazy band crossing the whole sky, but hidden in places by dark dust clouds.

Light from the center of
the Milky Way takes

26,000 years

to reach Earth

Studying space

For most of history, astronomers used only their eyes to observe the stars and planets in the night sky. The invention of the telescope in the 16th century opened up the skies for the astronomers. Today, they can study objects in space in far greater detail using a wide range of powerful telescopes and computers. Seen here is one of the four telescopes of the Very Large Telescope at the Paranal Observatory in Chile. It has fired a laser beam to guide its computer-controlled system for making the images sharper.

RADIO TELESCOPE
Radio telescopes, such as this APEX antenna, have huge curved dishes that collect radio waves from space.

How telescopes work

A telescope is an instrument that collects light—far more than a human eye can—from faraway objects and then magnifies them. Telescopes have evolved from simple models that could see nearby objects in space, such as the Moon, to powerful instruments that can detect light from stars billions of light-years away.

Optical telescopes

Optical telescopes mainly detect visible light. They have two main parts—an objective (or primary) lens or mirror, which collects and focuses light from a distant object, and an eyepiece to look at the image of the object. Most astronomical telescopes use mirrors.

Finder helps to target object for study

A **Newtonian telescope** is a simple type of optical telescope in which a primary mirror collects light from an object, which is then reflected to a secondary mirror. This directs the light to the eyepiece where a person sees a focused and magnified image.

Person sees magnified image through eyepiece

Primary mirror

Eyepiece

Objective is made of one or more lenses

Primary mirror reflects and focuses light onto the secondary mirror

Flat secondary mirror directs light to eyepiece

Light from distant object

Eyepiece

Light from distant object

Refractors are small telescopes that use lenses to refract, or bend, light rays. The lenses collect and focus light onto a small mirror, which bounces the image to the eyepiece.

Light bounces back
to eyepiece

Light from
distant object

Secondary
mirror

The **Schmidt-Cassegrain telescope** is a compact reflecting telescope. Its curved secondary mirror directs light to the eyepiece through a hole in the primary mirror. This design is popular for amateur telescopes because it has a short tube and is easy to use.

ADAPTIVE OPTICS

Moving air in the atmosphere blurs light from stars. Some large professional telescopes use a system called adaptive optics to fix this problem. They fire a laser beam to a height of about 60 miles (100 km), where it makes gas glow. Blurring of light from the gas is measured by a sensor and from this a computer learns how to adjust a special bendable mirror that reflects and sharpens up the images.

Radio telescopes

Radio telescopes can be tuned to particular radio wavelengths. They detect radio waves given off by objects in space and can convert the waves into images using computers. This radio image shows radio waves from jets shooting out of the center of a galaxy.

Ground-based telescopes

There are two types of telescope in modern Earth-based observatories: optical and radio. Almost all large optical telescopes use mirrors, not lenses, and detect both visible light and infrared radiation. Radio telescopes use metal dishes to focus radio waves from space onto receivers.

Keck

The twin Keck telescopes are two of the largest optical and infrared telescopes in the world. They use a technique called adaptive optics to fix a problem faced by all ground-based optical telescopes—distortion, or blurring, of light caused by moving air in the atmosphere.

LOCATION Mauna Kea, Hawaii

DIAMETER OF MAIN MIRROR 33 ft (10 m) each

TYPE Optical

DATE BUILT Keck I in 1993, Keck II in 1996

Gran Telescopio Canarias

Set at a high altitude of 7,440 ft (2,267 m) and in an area free of artificial lights, this telescope is ideally placed to observe the night sky. In 2012, it was the largest optical telescope in the world, and has been used to study planets outside the solar system.

LOCATION Roque de los Muchachos Observatory, La Palma, Canary Islands

DIAMETER OF MAIN MIRROR 34 ft (10.4 m)

TYPE Optical

DATE BUILT 2007

Large Binocular

The two main mirrors of the Large Binocular telescope work together to collect as much light as a single mirror with a diameter of 39 ft (11.8 m), and can pick out as much detail as a mirror 75 ft (22.8 m) wide.

LOCATION Mount Graham International Observatory, Arizona

DIAMETER OF MAIN MIRROR
27½ ft (8.4 m) each

TYPE Optical

DATE BUILT 2004

Very Large Telescope (VLT)

The Very Large Telescope consists of four units that can work on their own or together as one telescope. The individual telescopes can take images of objects four billion times fainter than can be seen with the naked eye. When working together, the telescopes allow astronomers to see objects 25 times fainter than those seen with the individual units.

LOCATION Paranal Observatory, Atacama Desert, Chile

DIAMETER OF MAIN MIRROR
27 ft (8.2 m) each

TYPE Optical

DATE BUILT First unit built in 1998

McMath-Pierce

This is the largest telescope for studying the Sun. It collects sunlight and directs it to an underground observation room using a mirror. One of its uses is studying sunspots—temporary cool regions on the visible surface of the Sun.

LOCATION Kitt Peak, Arizona

DIAMETER OF MAIN MIRROR 5¼ ft (1.6 m)

TYPE Optical

DATE BUILT 1962

Atacama Large Millimeter Array (ALMA)

The 66 antennae of this array work together as a highly sensitive telescope. Scientists use it to detect radiation from some of the coldest objects in the universe—giant clouds in some of the earliest and most distant galaxies. This radiation has a wavelength of about a millimeter—between that of infrared and radio waves—and is called millimeter radiation.

LOCATION Llano de Chajnantor Observatory, Atacama Desert, Chile

DIAMETER OF DISH 39 ft (12 m) (54 dishes) and 23 ft (7 m) (12 dishes)

TYPE Radio

DATE BUILT 2004–2012

Very Large Array (VLA)

Astronomers can link radio dishes to form an array, which collects more radio waves than a single dish. The Very Large Array has 27 dishes, which rest on tracks and can be moved to different positions. The dishes can be used individually, but detect much more detail when working together. Scientists have studied black holes using the VLA.

LOCATION National Radio Astronomy Observatory, New Mexico

DIAMETER OF DISH 82 ft (25 m) each

TYPE Radio

DATE BUILT 1980

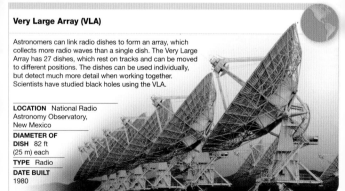

Arecibo

The Arecibo Observatory has the largest single-dish radio telescope in the world. The radio dish was built inside a natural depression in a valley. The telescope has helped make several important scientific breakthroughs, such as the discovery of the first planets outside the solar system.

LOCATION Arecibo, Puerto Rico

DIAMETER OF DISH 1,000 ft (305 m)

TYPE Radio

DATE BUILT 1963

Space telescopes

The atmosphere blocks some kinds of radiation, such as X-rays and gamma rays, but these can be studied by telescopes in space. It also blurs visible-light images, but this is not a problem in space, where telescopes can capture sharper, more detailed images.

Chandra X-ray Observatory

The Chandra is designed to observe X-rays from high-energy regions, such as the remains of exploded stars. The special mirrors in Chandra have been coated with iridium and gold to focus the X-rays.

DIAMETER OF MAIN MIRROR	4 ft (1.2 m)
TYPE	X-ray
DATE LAUNCHED	July 23, 1999
SIZE	45¼ ft (13.8 m) long

Spitzer Space Telescope

The Spitzer Space Telescope is the largest infrared observatory in space. It studies objects that mainly give off low-energy infrared radiation, or heat. These include small, dim stars, planets outside the solar system, and giant clouds in space.

DIAMETER OF MAIN MIRROR	
33 in (85 cm)	
TYPE	Optical
DATE LAUNCHED	August 25, 2003
SIZE	14¾ ft (4.5 m) long

Artist's impression of the Spitzer Space Telescope

Hubble Space Telescope

The Hubble Space Telescope orbits Earth about 350 miles (560 km) above the surface. It detects infrared, visible, and ultraviolet radiation from objects in space. This telescope has revealed much about the universe. It helped scientists to work out the rate at which the universe is expanding as well as the age of the universe—between 13 and 14 billion years. The Ultra Deep Field image (see pp. 114–115) taken by the Hubble Space Telescope is the most detailed visible-light image of the farthest reaches of the universe yet taken.

DIAMETER OF MAIN MIRROR
7¾ ft (2.4 m)

TYPE Optical

DATE LAUNCHED April 24, 1990

SIZE 42½ ft (12.9 m) long

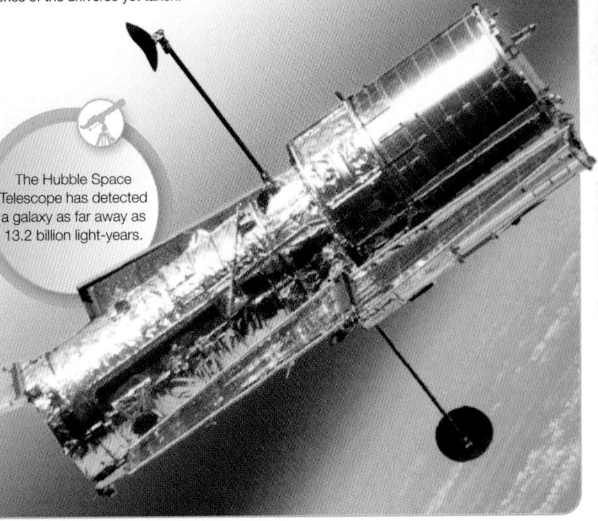

The Hubble Space Telescope has detected a galaxy as far away as 13.2 billion light-years.

The Hubble Space Telescope is
so sensitive
that if two candles were placed 6½ ft
(2 m) apart about 7,000 miles (11,265 km)
away, it would see them both separately

HUBBLE
The Hubble Space Telescope captured this image of bright young stars in a cluster called NGC 602. This star cluster lies in the Small Magellanic Cloud, a dwarf galaxy just outside our own. The telescope used its Advanced Camera for Surveys to take this incredibly detailed image.

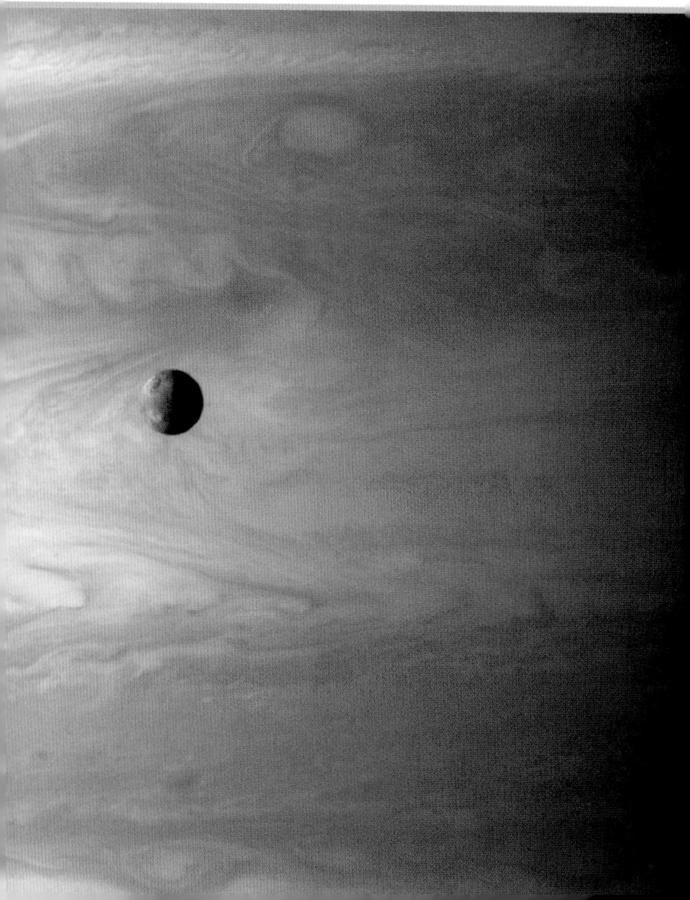

The solar system

The Sun's neighbors in space include eight planets, their moons, and countless smaller bodies made of rock or ice, such as dwarf planets, asteroids, and comets. All orbit the Sun, held in place by its gravity. Together, the Sun and all the objects that travel around it are known as the solar system. It formed around 5 billion years ago, not long after the Sun was born from a dense cloud of gas.

CRATERS
Craters pock-mark the surface of Earth's Moon. They were created when asteroids collided with the Moon in the past.

The Sun's family

About 4.6 billion years ago, the solar system began to form from a gigantic cloud of gas and dust. Over millions of years, gravity brought the gas and dust together, shrinking the cloud into a flat, spinning disk. The center of the disk heated up and formed the Sun. The material around the Sun formed clumps, which turned into planets, asteroids, moons, and comets.

Jupiter

Uranus

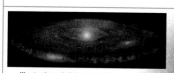

Illustration of disk around the young Sun

The solar system forms

Grains of dust and ice in the Sun's disk collided with each other and became stuck together. Near the Sun, chunks of rock collided with each other to form the rocky planets. In the outer part of the disk, gas collected around chunks of rock and ice, forming the giant gas planets. Many icy chunks were left over near the disk's edge.

Jupiter and its moon, Io

Giant planets
The four giant planets occupy the outer part of the solar system. Jupiter and Saturn are called gas giants because of their thick, gas-rich atmospheres. Uranus and Neptune are called ice giants because their atmospheres contain frozen methane.

The solar system

Orbiting the Sun are eight planets—Mercury, Venus, Earth, Mars, Jupiter, Saturn, Uranus, and Neptune—and trillions of smaller bodies: dwarf planets, moons, asteroids, comets, and meteoroids.

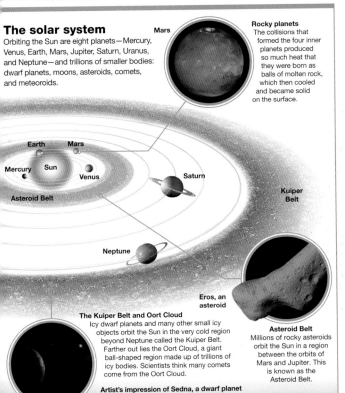

Rocky planets
The collisions that formed the four inner planets produced so much heat that they were born as balls of molten rock, which then cooled and became solid on the surface.

Mars

Earth
Mars

Mercury   Sun
Venus
Saturn

Asteroid Belt

Kuiper Belt

Neptune

Eros, an asteroid

The Kuiper Belt and Oort Cloud
Icy dwarf planets and many other small icy objects orbit the Sun in the very cold region beyond Neptune called the Kuiper Belt. Farther out lies the Oort Cloud, a giant ball-shaped region made up of trillions of icy bodies. Scientists think many comets come from the Oort Cloud.

Artist's impression of Sedna, a dwarf planet

Asteroid Belt
Millions of rocky asteroids orbit the Sun in a region between the orbits of Mars and Jupiter. This is known as the Asteroid Belt.

The rocky planets

The planets closest to the Sun—Mercury, Venus, Earth, and Mars—are called the rocky planets. They have solid crusts and are made mainly of rock and metal. They have few moons or none at all.

FOCUS ON...
ATMOSPHERE
An atmosphere is a layer of gases surrounding a planet, held in place by the planet's gravity.

Mercury

Mercury is the nearest planet to the Sun. The Sun bakes the side facing it to a blistering 806°F (430°C), while the night side freezes to −292°F (−180°C).

MAXIMUM DISTANCE FROM THE SUN
43.3 million miles (69.8 million km)

DIAMETER 3,030 miles (4,879 km)

YEAR LENGTH 88 Earth days

DAY LENGTH 58.6 Earth days

Venus

Venus is covered in thick clouds and its features are only visible using radar images such as the one below. The planet takes longer to spin on its axis than it does to orbit the Sun.

MAXIMUM DISTANCE FROM THE SUN
67.6 million miles (108.9 million km)

DIAMETER 7,520 miles (12,104 km)

YEAR LENGTH 224.7 Earth days

DAY LENGTH 243 Earth days

▲ Thick clouds of sulfur dioxide and sulfuric acid in Venus' atmosphere allow little sunlight to reach its surface.

▲ Gases in Earth's atmosphere scatter the blue light in sunlight more widely than red, making the sky appear blue.

▲ Mars' thin atmosphere is almost entirely carbon dioxide. Dust in the atmosphere makes the Martian sky look pink.

Earth

From space, Earth appears blue because of the oceans that cover most of its surface. They are no deeper than 7 miles (11 km), and a rocky crust forms the ocean floor.

MAXIMUM DISTANCE FROM THE SUN
94.5 million miles (152.6 million km)

DIAMETER 7,926 miles (12,756 km)

YEAR LENGTH 365.25 days

DAY LENGTH 23.9 hours

Mars

Mars' dusty soil contains iron oxide, which gives the planet its distinctive reddish color. Its surface features include a deep canyon system and a number of volcanoes.

MAXIMUM DISTANCE FROM THE SUN
154.8 million miles (249.2 million km)

DIAMETER 4,220 miles (6,792 km)

YEAR LENGTH 687 Earth days

DAY LENGTH 24.6 Earth hours

The giant planets

Beyond the inner planets lie the gigantic outer planets—Jupiter, Saturn, Uranus, and Neptune. Each has a core made of rock and ice, a dense atmosphere, and a large family of moons.

FOCUS ON...
RINGS
The outer planets all have rings made of dust, rock, and ice.

Jupiter

The largest planet in the solar system, Jupiter is so big that more than 1,300 Earths could fit inside it. Despite its large size, Jupiter spins faster than any other planet—so fast, in fact, that it bulges slightly at its equator and clouds in its atmosphere are pulled into thick bands. The top layer of the planet's atmosphere forms its visible surface.

MAXIMUM DISTANCE FROM THE SUN
507 million miles (816 million km)

DIAMETER
88,845 miles (142,984 km)

YEAR LENGTH
11.9 Earth years

DAY LENGTH
9.9 Earth hours

▲ Jupiter is surrounded by faint rings. This artist's impression shows the location of the rings above its equator.

▲ Twelve narrow rings made up of lanes of dust make up the ring system around Uranus. This image of the rings was captured over a long period of time and stars appear as short streaks.

Saturn

A spectacular series of rings makes Saturn a very distinctive planet. Saturn is mainly made up of gas and liquids and is less dense than any other planet in the solar system. Scientists think its atmosphere has three cloud layers, made up of ammonia, ammonium hydrosulfide, and water.

MAXIMUM DISTANCE FROM THE SUN
932 million miles (1.5 billion km)

DIAMETER 74,900 miles
(120,536 km)

YEAR LENGTH
29.5 Earth years

DAY LENGTH
10.7 Earth hours

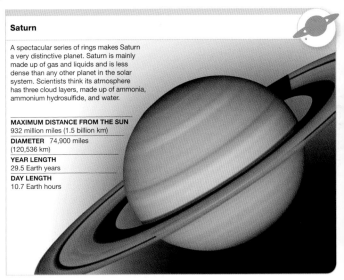

Uranus

While most planets spin like tops, pale blue Uranus spins on its side, like a rolling ball. It is likely that a collision with an asteroid caused the planet to tip over. From Earth, its faint rings appear to encircle the planet from top to bottom. The atmosphere of Uranus is mainly made up of hydrogen and helium with a small amount of methane and traces of water and ammonia.

MAXIMUM DISTANCE FROM THE SUN
1.86 billion miles (3 billion km)

DIAMETER 31,760 miles (51,118 km)

YEAR LENGTH 84 Earth years

DAY LENGTH 17.2 Earth hours

Neptune

The deep blue color of Neptune is caused by methane in its atmosphere. Winds in the atmosphere blow at up to 1,340 mph (2,160 kph), making it one of the windiest planets. Neptune is also one of the coldest planets in the solar system. The temperature at the top of its cloud layers is a freezing −330°F (−201°C).

MAXIMUM DISTANCE FROM THE SUN 2.8 billion miles (4.5 billion km)

DIAMETER 30,775 miles (49,528 km)

YEAR LENGTH
164.8 Earth years

DAY LENGTH
16.1 Earth hours

Great Dark Spot in Neptune's atmosphere

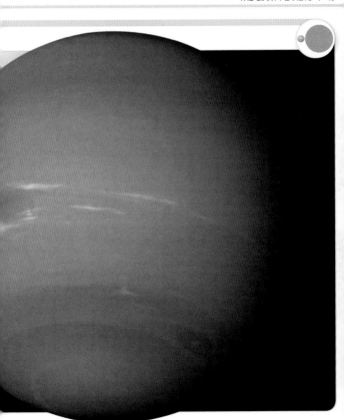

Planetary features

Telescopes and spacecraft have helped scientists study many of the features on the solar system's planets—from craters, mountains, and valleys on the inner planets to the intense storms and gigantic rings of the outer planets.

Caloris Basin
Mercury

This large basin, or plain, inside an enormous crater is bigger than the American state of Texas. It was formed after a large asteroid hit the planet, triggering powerful shock waves and a massive earthquake.

FEATURE TYPE Basin
SIZE 932 miles (1,500 km) across

Craters on basin floor

Brahms Crater
Mercury

The hilly circular walls of this crater have a series of stairlike formations on their slopes. This structure is typical of craters this size. Ejecta (debris released by impacts) have formed the hills along the rim of the crater.

FEATURE TYPE Impact crater
SIZE 61 miles (98 km) across

Discovery Rupes
Mercury

Discovery Rupes is the longest of the series of 16 clifflike ridges discovered on the surface of Mercury. It was formed when part of Mercury's rocky crust cracked and was pushed up early in the planet's life.

FEATURE TYPE	Ridge
SIZE	310 miles (500 km) long

Discovery Rupes cuts through craters

Mead Crater
Venus

Mead, the largest crater on Venus, is made up of multiple rings. The asteroid impact that formed the crater either melted rocks in the region or caused lava (molten rocks) to spill out from below the surface. This formed a shallow basin inside the crater after the molten material cooled.

FEATURE TYPE	Multiringed impact crater
SIZE	174 miles (280 km) across

Maat Mons
Venus

Hundreds of volcanoes cover the surface of Venus and it is possible that some of them are still active. Maat Mons is the largest of these volcanoes and its base is surrounded by lava flows that stretch out for hundreds of miles.

FEATURE TYPE	Shield volcano (shield-shaped volcano)
SIZE	5 miles (8 km) high

Ishtar Terra
Venus

Seen here in a false-color image, Ishtar Terra is one of the two main highlands (elevated or mountainous regions) on Venus. It is about the size of Australia and stands 2 miles (3.3 km) above the surrounding area.

FEATURE TYPE Highland

SIZE 3,485 miles (5,610 km) long

Addams Crater
Venus

This unique crater has a long tail of lava and debris to one side. It was created when an asteroid hit the ground, flinging ejecta (debris released by impacts) over one side of the crater. The lava and ejecta stretch from the rim to form a fishlike shape toward the east of the crater.

Eistla Regio
Venus

This highland was first viewed by the *Pioneer* Venus orbiter in the 1980s. Eistla Regio lies in the planet's equatorial region (area around the equator). Prominent features on this terrain include volcanoes, such as Gula Mons and Sif Mons.

FEATURE TYPE Volcanic highland

SIZE 4,980 miles (8,015 km) long

Gula mons is the larger of the two volcanoes on Eistla Regio

Lava flows stretch for hundreds of miles

FEATURE TYPE Impact crater

SIZE 56 miles (90 km) across

Sapas Mons
Venus

Like many other volcanoes on Venus, Sapas Mons is shaped like a shield or an upturned plate, with a broad base and gently sloping sides. The volcano has two mesas (elevated areas with flat tops) on a single summit.

FEATURE TYPE Shield volcano

SIZE 1 mile (1.5 km) high

Mesa on summit

The circular, flat-topped volcanoes on Eistla Regio are called pancake domes.

Himalayas
Earth

Earth's crust (outer shell) is made up of sections called plates that move very slowly. Between 50 and 30 million years ago, plate movements caused a landmass—now known as India—to collide with Southeast Asia. This collision formed the Himalayas—the tallest mountain range on the planet. These mountains continue to rise even today, although at a very slow rate of 20 in (50 cm) every 100 years.

FEATURE TYPE Mountain range

SIZE 2,400 miles (3,800 km) long

Antarctic ice sheet
Earth

A giant mass of ice covers almost the entire continent of Antarctica in Earth's southern polar region. This sheet of ice holds more than 70 percent of Earth's fresh water and is 3 miles (4.5 km) thick in some places.

FEATURE TYPE
Continental ice sheet

SIZE
5.3 million sq miles
(13.7 million sq km)
in area

Barringer Crater
Earth

This crater in Arizona was formed around 50,000 years ago when the Canyon Diablo meteorite, a chunk of nickel-iron about 165 ft (50 m) wide, hit Earth. The force of the impact melted most of the meteorite and millions of tons of sandstone and limestone were blasted out in every direction.

FEATURE TYPE Impact crater

SIZE 4,000 ft (1,200 m) across

Sahara Desert
Earth

Earth's largest hot desert, the Sahara covers nearly 10 percent of the African continent. Winds blowing over the desert create sand dunes, which can be as tall as 1,000 ft (300 m). This region receives little or no rainfall.

FEATURE TYPE Desert

SIZE 3.5 million sq miles (9 million sq km) in area

Nile River
Earth

The Nile is the longest river on Earth. Although it flows mostly through desert on its way to the Mediterranean Sea in the north, sediment carried by the Nile creates fertile farmland along its banks.

FEATURE TYPE River

SIZE 4,131 miles (6,648 km) long

The fertile sediment deposited at the mouth of the Nile forms its triangular delta

Olympus Mons
Mars

The tallest mountain in the solar system, Olympus Mons rises to a height of 15 miles (24 km). It is a large shield volcano (a broad volcano with shallow slopes) with a volume 50 times that of any shield volcano on Earth.

FEATURE TYPE Shield volcano

SIZE 388 miles (624 km) in diameter

The summit has six calderas (collapsed craters)

Victoria Crater
Mars

The high ridges around the rim of this impact crater give it an unusual scalloplike shape. Erosion of the rim has caused the wall material to crumble and fall inward, forming bays. The inner wall of the crater is made of layers of exposed sedimentary rocks. These rocks form over many years by the joining together of little pieces of rock and sand, carried by air or water. The crater floor is covered with a field of sand dunes.

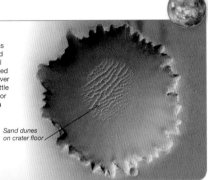

Sand dunes on crater floor

FEATURE TYPE Impact crater

SIZE ½ mile (800 m) wide

Valles Marineris
Mars

Valles Marineris is named after the *Mariner 9* orbiter, which sent back the first images of the gorge in 1971–72. The feature consists of canyons stretching for more than 2,500 miles (4,000 km). It is the largest feature formed by tectonic movements (activity of plates in a planet's crust) on Mars. Many of the canyons are five times deeper than the Grand Canyon in Arizona.

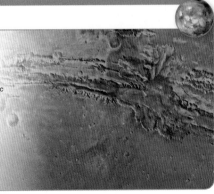

FEATURE TYPE Series of canyons

SIZE More than 2,500 miles (4,000 km) long

Great Red Spot
Jupiter

The Great Red Spot in Jupiter's atmosphere is an enormous storm that had been raging for at least 340 years when it was first observed by astronomers. Twice the size of Earth, it is the largest known storm in the solar system.

FEATURE TYPE Storm

SIZE 15,000–25,000 miles (24,000–40,000 km) across

Rings of Saturn
Saturn

The spectacular rings of Saturn are actually a band of icy chunks orbiting this gas giant. These chunks range in size from grains of dust to boulders that are several yards wide. They act like mirrors and reflect sunlight, making the rings very bright.

FEATURE TYPE Rings

SIZE 8 million miles (12.9 million km) wide

Dragon Storm
Saturn

Called the Dragon Storm because of its monstrous shape, this vast thunderstorm in Saturn's atmosphere was spotted in 2004–05 in a region called Storm Alley, which is home to many other storms.

Dragon Storm

FEATURE TYPE Storm

SIZE 2,175 miles (3,500 km) from north to south

Great Dark Spot
Neptune

In 1989, this great storm was first observed in Neptune's atmosphere by the *Voyager 2* spacecraft and was found to be as large as Earth. It had disappeared by the time the Hubble Space Telescope observed Neptune in 1994.

FEATURE TYPE Storm

SIZE 8,100 miles (13,000 km) across

Great Dark Spot

MARTIAN VALLEY
Candor Chasma is one of the largest valleys of
the Valles Marineris canyon system on Mars. Seen
here is an artist's impression of the valley. Some
scientists think that the valley formed due to
movements of plates in the Martian crust.

Russian scientists hope to send a

manned expedition

to Mars by the year 2020

The Moon

The only natural satellite of the Earth, the Moon is our planet's closest neighbor. It is a lifeless ball of rock with almost no atmosphere. Its surface is mottled with impact craters caused by asteroids and comets over the last 4.5 billion years.

FOCUS ON...
SIDES

The Moon completes one rotation on its axis in the same time that it revolves once around Earth and so keeps one side facing Earth at all times.

▲ The near side of the Moon is the face that can always be seen from Earth.

▲ The Moon's far side is hidden from Earth. It was first photographed by the *Luna 3* spacecraft in 1959.

Taurus-Littrow Valley

This feature lies near the Taurus Mountains and to the south of Littrow Crater. The valley is surrounded by steep-sided mountains called massifs, which are the remains of old crater walls. It was the landing site for *Apollo 17*, the last manned mission to the Moon.

FEATURE TYPE	Valley
SIZE	18.6 miles (30 km) across
AGE	About 3.85 billion years old

Mare Tranquillitatis

Mare Tranquillitatis, or "Sea of Tranquility," was the landing site for the first manned mission to the Moon. A mare is a large, relatively flat area, created by enormous lava flows.

FEATURE TYPE Lunar sea (basin, or plain)

SIZE 542 miles (873 km) across

AGE About 3.6 billion years old

Copernicus Crater

Huge terraced walls line this young crater. Fine gray rocks thrown out when the crater was formed have created streaks, called rays, around the crater. Some of these rocks were collected by astronauts on the *Apollo 12* mission.

FEATURE TYPE Impact crater

SIZE 57 miles (91 km) across

AGE About 900 million years old

Montes Apenninus

The mountains in this range form the southwestern border of a basin called Mare Imbrium. Montes Apenninus was created when the asteroid impact that formed this mare triggered shock waves, which lifted parts of the Moon's crust.

FEATURE TYPE Mountain range

SIZE 370 miles (600 km) long

AGE About 3.9 billion years old

Moons

There are at least 175 moons orbiting the planets and dwarf planets in the solar system. Some of these moons are pock-marked with craters, while others are covered in ice. They range in size from tiny Phobos to gigantic Ganymede.

Phobos
Mars

Phobos is closer to its parent planet than any other moon in the solar system. It orbits Mars at a speed of more than 1.2 miles (2 km) every second. Martian gravity is gradually tugging on Phobos and will tear it apart in about 7.6 million years.

SIZE 16.6 miles (26.8 km) across

MAXIMUM DISTANCE FROM PLANET 5,830 miles (9,380 km)

TIME TAKEN TO ORBIT PLANET 7.65 Earth hours

Ganymede
Jupiter

The largest moon in the solar system, Ganymede is even larger than Mercury. Its surface is a crust of ice floating on top of many layers of partly melted ice. Beneath them, layers of rock surround an iron core.

SIZE 3,270 miles (5,262 km) across

MAXIMUM DISTANCE FROM PLANET 664,870 miles (1.07 million km)

TIME TAKEN TO ORBIT PLANET 7.15 Earth days

Deimos
Mars

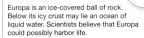

This moon has the diameter of a large city and is composed of carbon-rich rock. Its surface is covered in a layer of loose rock and dust. Scientists think that it may have been an asteroid that was captured by Martian gravity.

SIZE 9.3 miles (15 km) across

MAXIMUM DISTANCE FROM PLANET 14,600 miles (23,500 km) across

TIME TAKEN TO ORBIT PLANET 30.3 Earth hours

Europa
Jupiter

Europa is an ice-covered ball of rock. Below its icy crust may lie an ocean of liquid water. Scientists believe that Europa could possibly harbor life.

SIZE 1,940 miles (3,122 km) across

MAXIMUM DISTANCE FROM PLANET 416,878 miles (670,900 km)

TIME TAKEN TO ORBIT PLANET 3.55 Earth days

The purple color in this false color image shows frost near a pole

Callisto
Jupiter

There are no mountains or volcanoes on Callisto. Its dark crust is one of the most heavily cratered of any body in the solar system. Large multiringed basins, ridges, and fractures also dot its surface.

SIZE 2,995 miles (4,820 km) across
MAXIMUM DISTANCE FROM PLANET
1.17 million miles (1.88 million km)
TIME TAKEN TO ORBIT PLANET
16.69 Earth days

Ice on crater rims and ridges shines brightly

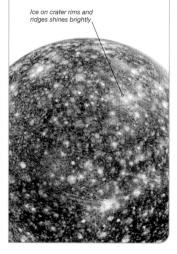

Io
Jupiter

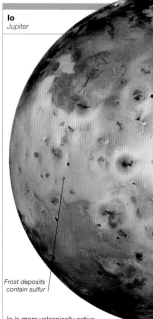

Frost deposits contain sulfur

Io is more volcanically active than any other moon or planet in the solar system. Jupiter is mainly responsible for this—its gravity raises strong tides throughout Io. These tides generate energy in Io's interior, which heats the rocks there and melts them. The molten rocks erupt from volcanoes all over the moon's surface.

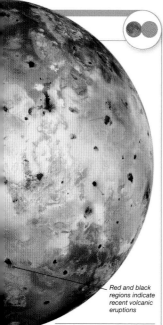

Red and black regions indicate recent volcanic eruptions

SIZE 2,260 miles (3,643 km) across

MAXIMUM DISTANCE FROM PLANET
261,800 miles (421,600 km)

TIME TAKEN TO ORBIT PLANET
1.77 Earth days

Titan
Saturn

Saturn's largest moon, Titan, is the only moon with a thick atmosphere. Its surface is hidden under orange haze in the nitrogen atmosphere but radar maps have revealed lakes of liquid ethane and methane.

SIZE 3,200 miles (5,150 km) across

MAXIMUM DISTANCE FROM PLANET
758,070 miles (1.22 million km)

TIME TAKEN TO ORBIT PLANET
15.95 Earth days

Infrared image of Titan

Mimas
Saturn

Covered with craters, Mimas is the smallest of Saturn's large moons and the closest to the planet. Its most prominent feature is a giant impact crater called Herschel.

SIZE 260 miles (418 km) across

MAXIMUM DISTANCE FROM PLANET
115,277 miles (185,520 km)

TIME TAKEN TO ORBIT PLANET
0.94 Earth days

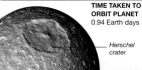

Herschel crater

Enceladus
Saturn

There are four long fissures (long, deep cracks on the surface) called "tiger stripes" near the south pole of Enceladus. Plumes of water vapor regularly spray out from the moon's surface through these fissures. The water-ice surface of this moon reflects more than 90 percent of the sunlight hitting it, making Enceladus one of the brightest objects in the solar system.

SIZE 318 miles
(512 km) across

**MAXIMUM DISTANCE
FROM PLANET**
147,900 miles
(238,020 km)

**TIME TAKEN TO ORBIT
PLANET**
1.37 Earth days

*Fissure on
moon's surface*

Hyperion
Saturn

Icy Hyperion is dotted by so many deep craters that it looks like an enormous sponge in space. On another moon, a meteoroid impact would blast out debris from the hard surface. The debris would then fall back, filling in any surrounding craters. However, Hyperion's icy surface is not as hard as that of other moons. It is brittle and shatters easily, and so a meteoroid striking it creates a hole, but does not produce much debris to fill the craters.

SIZE 230 miles (370 km) across

MAXIMUM DISTANCE FROM PLANET
919,620 miles (1.48 million km)

TIME TAKEN TO ORBIT PLANET
21.28 Earth days

Rhea
Saturn

Rhea is Saturn's second largest moon. It always shows the same face to Saturn, just as the Moon's near side always faces Earth. Around three-quarters of Rhea is made of ice, while the rest is rock.

SIZE 949 miles
(1,528 km) across

**MAXIMUM DISTANCE
FROM PLANET**
327,490 miles
(527,040 km)

**TIME TAKEN TO
ORBIT PLANET**
4.5 Earth days

Tethys
Saturn

This moon shares its orbit around Saturn with two tiny moons: Calypso and Telesto. A major feature on its surface is a crater called Odysseus, about 250 miles (400 km) in diameter.

SIZE 666 miles (1,072 km) across

MAXIMUM DISTANCE FROM PLANET
183,100 miles (294,660 km)

TIME TAKEN TO ORBIT PLANET 1.9 Earth days

Iapetus
Saturn

This moon has two contrasting sides. One side is as dark as coal, while the other (seen here) is brighter. Scientist think that the surface of the darker side is coated in a material made of carbon.

SIZE 914 miles (1,471 km) across

MAXIMUM DISTANCE FROM PLANET
2.2 million miles (3.5 million km)

TIME TAKEN TO ORBIT PLANET
79.33 Earth days

Miranda
Uranus

Many different kinds of surface feature seem to be glued together at odd angles on this moon. Scientists believe this is because of large asteroids striking the moon, which caused partly molten ice to rise to its rock-ice surface and refreeze, forming the canyons, cliffs, and valleys.

SIZE 300 miles
(480 km) across

**MAXIMUM DISTANCE
FROM PLANET**
80,400 miles
(129,390 km)

**TIME TAKEN TO
ORBIT PLANET**
1.4 Earth days

Oberon
Uranus

This is the second largest moon of Uranus. Its surface is pitted with far more impact craters than Uranus's other moons. The largest crater, called Hamlet, is about 184 miles (296 km) wide.

SIZE 946 miles
(1,523 km) across

**MAXIMUM DISTANCE
FROM PLANET**
362,580 miles
(583,520 km)

**TIME TAKEN TO
ORBIT PLANET**
13.5 Earth days

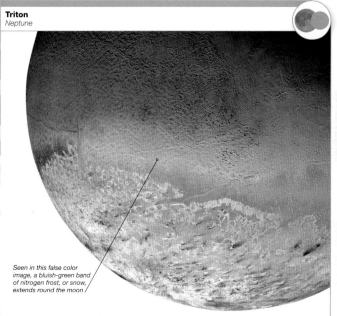

Triton
Neptune

Seen in this false color image, a bluish-green band of nitrogen frost, or snow, extends round the moon

Triton's surface is made of frozen nitrogen, water, and carbon dioxide and the temperature at the surface can drop to −391°F (−235°C). Tiny amounts of ice evaporate to make a thin atmosphere. Triton is the only large moon in the solar system to orbit in a direction opposite to its parent planet's spin.

SIZE 1,680 miles (2,707 km) across

MAXIMUM DISTANCE FROM PLANET
220,438 miles (354,760 km)

TIME TAKEN TO ORBIT PLANET
5.88 Earth days

Dwarf planets

These almost-round bodies orbit the Sun, but are too small to be considered planets. One, Ceres, lies in the Asteroid Belt between Mars and Jupiter, while the other four found, so far, lie beyond Neptune in the Kuiper Belt.

Pluto

From 1930 to 2006, Pluto was considered a planet. The discovery of a larger rocky body called Eris in 2005 led scientists to reclassify Pluto as a dwarf planet. Not much is known about this icy world. It has a surface temperature of −382°F (−230°C). Pluto's long elliptical orbit means that, for 20 years in every orbit, it is closer to the Sun than Neptune.

MAXIMUM DISTANCE FROM THE SUN 4.5 billion miles (7.3 billion km)

SIZE Around 1,430 miles (2,304 km) in diameter

TIME TAKEN TO ORBIT THE SUN 248 Earth years

Haumea

Haumea rotates faster than most large objects in the solar system. It takes just four hours to complete one spin on its axis. Over thousands of years, its fast spin has given it a stretched, oval shape. Haumea's moons, Namaka and Hi'iaka, are also irregular in shape and were discovered in 2005.

MAXIMUM DISTANCE FROM THE SUN
4.78 billion miles (7.7 billion km)

SIZE 870 miles (1,400 km) average diameter

TIME TAKEN TO ORBIT THE SUN 282 Earth years

Artist's impression of Haumea and its moons

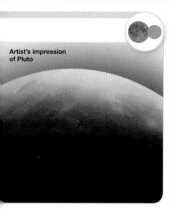

**Artist's impression
of Pluto**

Ceres

In 1801, Ceres became the first object
to be discovered in the Asteroid Belt. It is the
largest object in this region, and accounts for
one-third of the entire mass of the belt.

MAXIMUM DISTANCE FROM THE SUN
277 million miles (446 million km)

SIZE 580 miles (930 km) in diameter

TIME TAKEN TO ORBIT THE SUN
4.6 Earth years

Artist's impression of Ceres

Eris

This is one of the largest dwarf planets
in the solar system. In parts of its orbit, Eris
is more than twice as distant from the Sun as
Pluto. It has a small moon called Dysnomia.

MAXIMUM DISTANCE FROM THE SUN
9.07 billion miles (14.6 billion km)

SIZE Around 1,445 miles (2,326 km) in diameter

TIME TAKEN TO ORBIT THE SUN 561 Earth years

Asteroids

Millions of small rocky objects left over from when the solar system formed are called asteroids. Most are found in a wide, circular region between the orbits of Mars and Jupiter called the Asteroid Belt.

Eros

In 2001, this became the first asteroid to be orbited by a spacecraft—the *NEAR Shoemaker* craft studied it for about a year. The highly reflective surface of this peanut-shaped lump of rock is covered by a blanket of dust and rock fragments.

MAXIMUM DISTANCE FROM THE SUN
136 million miles (218 million km)

SIZE 21.4 miles (34.4 km) long

TIME TAKEN TO ORBIT THE SUN
1.76 Earth years

ASTEROID TYPE S-type

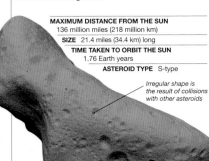

Irregular shape is the result of collisions with other asteroids

Vesta

Vesta reflects much of the sunlight it receives, making it the brightest asteroid in the night sky and the only one visible to the naked eye. It is also one of the largest asteroids in the solar system.

MAXIMUM DISTANCE FROM THE SUN 219 million miles (353 million km)

SIZE 348 miles (560 km) in diameter

TIME TAKEN TO ORBIT THE SUN 3.63 Earth years

ASTEROID TYPE V-type

Gaspra

This silicate-rich asteroid has hundreds of small craters on its gray surface. The spacecraft *Galileo* imaged around 80 percent of Gaspra's surface when it flew by in 1991.

MAXIMUM DISTANCE FROM THE SUN 206 million miles (331 million km)

SIZE 11.2 miles (18 km) long

TIME TAKEN TO ORBIT THE SUN 3.29 Earth years

ASTEROID TYPE S-type

Ida

The *Galileo* spacecraft studied Ida in detail in 1993. Amazingly, it found Ida to have its own tiny moon, which was named Dactyl. It was the first asteroid found to possess a moon. Ida is covered with worn craters, which suggest that it is quite old.

MAXIMUM DISTANCE FROM THE SUN 266 million miles (428 million km)

SIZE 37 miles (60 km) long

TIME TAKEN TO ORBIT THE SUN 4.84 Earth years

ASTEROID TYPE S-type

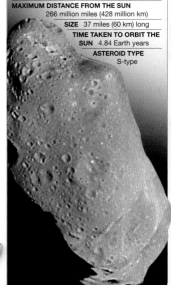

Comets

These chunks of rock and ice are remains of material left behind when the solar system formed. There are about 1 trillion comets in the Oort Cloud—a vast cloud surrounding the solar system far beyond the planets.

FOCUS ON...
STRUCTURE
Comets have an icy center, called the nucleus, and form tails of gas and dust near the Sun.

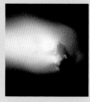

▲ The nucleus is a dirty snowball made of water ice and frozen gases. Heat from sunlight turns the ice and gases into vapor, forming a cloud around the nucleus.

▲ The heat also produces two tails pointing away from the Sun—one made of dust, the other of gas.

Halley

Halley's comet was the first periodic comet (a comet that takes less than 200 years to complete an orbit) to be identified. It was originally spotted by ancient Chinese astronomers around 240 BCE and has since been observed and studied about 30 times. The *Giotto* spacecraft visited it in 1986 and captured the first ever images of a comet's nucleus.

CLOSEST APPROACH TO THE SUN
55 million miles (88 million km)

NUCLEUS SIZE 7 miles (11 km) across

TIME TAKEN TO ORBIT THE SUN 76 Earth years

McNaught

This comet was discovered in 2006 and spotted in the skies of the southern hemisphere in January and February 2007. It was the brightest comet seen in the southern skies since the 1960s. Its orbit has now taken it far from the Sun and Earth and it will not return for tens of thousands of years.

CLOSEST APPROACH TO THE SUN
746 million miles (1.2 billion km)

NUCLEUS SIZE   15 miles (25 km) across

TIME TAKEN TO ORBIT THE SUN
92,600 Earth years

Shoemaker–Levy 9

At the time of its discovery, Shoemaker–Levy 9 was found to be orbiting Jupiter. The gas giant's gravity had captured the comet from its orbit around the Sun, and finally ripped it apart into 22 pieces when the comet passed close to Jupiter. The pieces (seen below) crashed into the planet.

AVERAGE DISTANCE FROM JUPITER
56,000 miles (90,000 km)

NUCLEUS SIZE   5 miles (8 km) across

TIME TAKEN TO ORBIT JUPITER
2.03 Earth years

Meteorites

Meteoroids are lumps of rock, dust, or ice that break off from asteroids or comets and start circling the Sun in new orbits. Some may fall toward Earth. Those that burn up in the atmosphere are called meteors, creating streaks of light across the sky called shooting stars. Those that reach Earth's surface are called meteorites.

Hoba West

Not only is this the largest meteorite to have been found on Earth, it is also the largest piece of naturally occurring iron on the planet's surface. It has not been moved because of its weight. It still lies at the spot where it landed and has become a tourist attraction.

MASS	66 tons (60 metric tons)
LOCATION	Grootfontein, Namibia
CONTENT	Nickel–iron

Canyon Diablo

This meteorite hit Earth to form the Barringer Crater (see pp.48–49) in Arizona. The force of the impact explosion was about 150 times greater than the atom bomb that destroyed Hiroshima in Japan in 1945 at the end of World War II. Many pieces of the meteorite have been found near the crater and many more chunks are likely to be buried under its rim.

MASS 30 tons (27 metric tons)

LOCATION Arizona

CONTENT Nickel–iron

Nakhla

The Nakhla meteorite landed in Egypt in a shower of stones on June 28, 1911, and was probably part of a larger chunk of rock that broke apart in the atmosphere. This volcanic rock is 1.2 billion years old.

MASS 88 lb (40 kg)

LOCATION Alexandria, Egypt

CONTENT Volcanic minerals

Black, glassy crust formed as the rock burned when shooting through Earth's atmosphere

Mundrabilla

Mundrabilla was the name given to a meteorite that broke up in the atmosphere millions of years ago, pieces of which have been found in Australia.

MASS 18 tons (16 metric tons)

LOCATION Nullarbor Plain, Western Australia

CONTENT Nickel–iron and iron–sulfide

Cross-section of a piece of the Mundrabilla meteorite

Stars and nebulae

The Carina Nebula (left), like other nebulae, is a gigantic cloud of gas and dust. In the dense parts of some nebulae, gravity pulls the dust and gas together to form clumps. As each clump forms, it heats up, becoming a star—a glowing ball of hot gas. Stars can shine for billions of years but do not live forever. At the end of their lives, many stars give birth to new nebulae, either by shedding their outer layers slowly as red giants or exploding suddenly as supernovae.

STAR CLUSTER
Globular clusters, such as 47 Tucanae, each contain hundreds of thousands of stars some of which are among the oldest known stars in our galaxy.

Life cycle of a star

Stars are massive balls of plasma, or glowing gas, powered by a process called nuclear fusion, which makes them shine. The life cycle of a star depends on its mass. A Sun-sized star can shine for billions of years, while stars with greater mass burn out faster and have shorter lives.

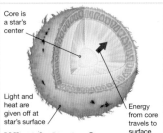

Core is a star's center

Light and heat are given off at star's surface

Energy from core travels to surface

What is a star?

A star is a giant ball of very hot gas—mainly hydrogen and helium—held together by its gravity. Inside its core, hydrogen atoms collide to form helium. This process is called nuclear fusion and it powers the star.

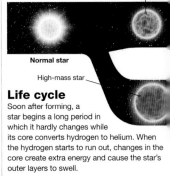

Star with Sunlike mass

Normal star

High-mass star

Life cycle

Soon after forming, a star begins a long period in which it hardly changes while its core converts hydrogen to helium. When the hydrogen starts to run out, changes in the core create extra energy and cause the star's outer layers to swell.

Star magnitude

A star's luminosity, or actual brightness, is the amount of energy it gives off per second. How bright a star appears from Earth is called its apparent magnitude. This depends on both the star's luminosity and its distance from Earth, so even a very luminous star may appear faint in the night sky if it is very far away.

As the core runs out of hydrogen, the star begins to swell. The core makes energy by fusing helium as well as hydrogen.

As the star swells, it begins to shed its outer layers. The star is now known as a **red giant**.

The shed layers form a shell of gas and dust, called a planetary nebula, around the remains of the star, which become a **white dwarf**.

The white dwarf dims and fades into a **black dwarf**.

If the core is between 1.5–3 times as massive as the Sun, it shrinks and turns into a **neutron star**.

Star expands to form a **red supergiant** after hydrogen runs out in the core.

The supergiant explodes as a **supernova** and blows off its outer layers, leaving behind only its core, which begins to shrink.

If the core is more than three times as massive as the Sun, it becomes highly dense and shrinks into a **black hole**. This appears black because even light cannot escape its strong gravity. Active black holes are circled by a ring of dust and gas and blowtorchlike jets of gas stream from their poles.

FOCUS ON...

Stars

The trillions of stars in space differ in size, mass, temperature, and brightness. The brightness of some stars, called variable stars, varies with time. Some form families of two or more stars orbiting each other—these are called multiple stars.

COLOR
The temperature of a star is reflected by its color, which may range from cool red to hot blue.

▲ Blue stars, such as Regulus, are the hottest. Its surface is at 22,000°F (12,000°C).

▲ Viewed from outside the atmosphere, the Sun's surface at 9,900°F (5,500°C) is pinkish white.

▲ Betelgeuse appears orange-red and is far cooler than the Sun at 5,800°F (3,200°C).

Proxima Centauri
Red dwarf

Based on its size, a star may be called a dwarf, giant, or supergiant. Small, cool stars called red dwarfs make up the majority of stars in the Milky Way. Proxima Centauri is a red dwarf—it is far smaller than the Sun and about 18,000 times fainter when viewed from Earth. It is the nearest star to the Sun.

COLOR	Orange-red
SIZE	0.14 times the Sun's diameter
CONSTELLATION	Centaurus
DISTANCE	4.4 light-years

Fomalhaut
White normal star

In the 1980s, scientists studying this star with a satellite called IRAS discovered a disk of ice and dust around it. They believed that planets might eventually be found orbiting Fomalhaut. In 2008, the Hubble Space Telescope spotted a blob near Fomalhaut that might be a planet.

COLOR White

SIZE 1.8 times the Sun's diameter

CONSTELLATION Piscis Austrinus

DISTANCE 25.1 light-years

Sirius A
White normal star

This star gets its name from the Greek word for "scorching." Sirius A is the brightest star in the night sky—it is one of the closest stars to Earth and it gives off about 25 times as much energy as the Sun.

COLOR White

SIZE 1.7 times the Sun's diameter

CONSTELLATION Canis Major

DISTANCE 8.6 light-years

Altair
White normal star

Altair rotates rapidly, making a full turn once every 6.5 hours and spinning at speeds of about 559,000 mph (900,000 kph). This has caused the star to bulge outward at its equator, while its poles have flattened. In comparison to Altair, the Sun spins at a speed of only 4,300 mph (6,900 kph).

COLOR White

SIZE 1.6 times the Sun's diameter

CONSTELLATION Aquila

DISTANCE 16.8 light-years

Vega
White normal star

Vega appears as the fifth brightest star in the night sky. It is a blue-tinged white star, with a surface temperature of about 16,772°F (9,300°C). After the Sun, it was the second star to be photographed.

COLOR White

SIZE 2.3 times the Sun's diameter

CONSTELLATION Lyra

DISTANCE 25.3 light-years

Polaris
Multiple star

The North star, or Polaris, lies close to the celestial north pole (see p.16). It appears almost still in the northern skies while other stars move as Earth spins on its axis. Polaris is actually a multiple star system made up of the giant Polaris A and two normal stars, all yellowish-white.

COLOR Yellowish-white

NUMBER OF STARS 3

CONSTELLATION Ursa Minor

DISTANCE 434 light-years

Rigel
Multiple star

Rigel, meaning "foot" in Arabic, gets its name from its position at the foot of the Orion constellation. This system consists of the blue supergiant Rigel A, which is twice as hot as the Sun and shines 85,000 times more brightly, and a fainter pair of normal blue-white stars—Rigel B and C.

COLOR Blue-white

NUMBER OF STARS 3

CONSTELLATION Orion

DISTANCE 860 light-years

15 Monocerotis
Blue-white variable star

The hot blue star 15 Monocerotis (also called S Monocerotis) is an example of a variable star. Its brightness varies over time by a small amount, with no particular pattern. It is actually two similar stars orbiting very close to each other, which are about 12 and 18 times more massive than the Sun. Together they are 217,000 times as bright as the Sun and they light up the nearby Cone Nebula.

COLOR	Blue-white
SIZE	Each 10–20 times the Sun's diameter
CONSTELLATION	Monoceros
DISTANCE	2,500 light-years

Mira A
Red giant, variable

Pulsating variable stars expand and contract at regular intervals, getting hotter and brighter as they contract. The red giant Mira A is a pulsating variable. It dims over a period of 330 days, eventually becoming too faint to be seen with the naked eye, before brightening again. It sheds material while zipping through the Milky Way at more than 291,000 mph (468,300 kph).

COLOR	Red
SIZE	Giant
CONSTELLATION	Cetus
DISTANCE	418 light-years

Ultraviolet image shows the 13-light-year-long tail made up of hot material shed by Mira

Mira

Star clusters

Some stars are in groups called clusters. Open clusters are loose groups of young stars that were born around the same time in a nebula and are not bound to each other very strongly. Old stars can be bound together very strongly by gravity into tight spheres called globular clusters.

Pleiades
Open cluster

Many open clusters are found along the Milky Way's spiral arms. The Pleiades, a 100-million-year-old open star cluster, is about 90 light-years in diameter. It contains bright blue stars and many dim brown dwarfs—objects with too little mass to be real stars.

NUMBER OF STARS	More than 1,000
CONSTELLATION	Taurus
DISTANCE	440 light-years

Omega Centauri
Globular cluster

Globular clusters orbit a galaxy and are found above or below the plane, or disk, of the galaxy. Omega Centauri is the brightest and largest of all the globular clusters near the Milky Way. It contains more than 10 million stars, which are packed so tightly together that people used to think it was a single star. The Hubble Space Telescope made it possible to study its stars in much more detail than before. This star cluster is about 12 billion years old.

NUMBER OF STARS	About 10 million
CONSTELLATION	Centaurus
DISTANCE	17,000 light-years

Jewel Box
Open cluster

The Jewel Box, or the Kappa Crucis Cluster, is a young cluster of about 100 stars. Three of its brightest stars are blue giants, while the fourth is a red supergiant. The Jewel Box is visible only from the southern hemisphere.

NUMBER OF STARS About 100

CONSTELLATION Crux

DISTANCE 8,150 light-years

Nine hot, young, blue stars

in the Pleiades are named after the titan, Atlas of Greek mythology, his wife, and their seven daughters

THE PLEIADES
This bright star cluster contains several hundred stars. Though often called "The Seven Sisters" in English, most people can only see six of its stars with the naked eye. A small telescope reveals many more than seven.

Exoplanets

Planets found outside the solar system are called extrasolar planets, or exoplanets. For many centuries, astronomers had suspected that planets orbited alien stars. The first exoplanet orbiting a sunlike star was found in 1995. Astronomers have now found hundreds of exoplanets and are discovering more all the time.

Kepler 11's planets

Six planets have been found orbiting the yellow dwarf star Kepler 11. Some of them are rocky, while the others are mainly made of gas. These planets are very close to Kepler 11 — more than twice as close as Earth is to our Sun.

NUMBER OF PLANETS 6

CONSTELLATION Cygnus

DISTANCE 2,000 light-years

Artist's impression of Kepler 11

Kepler 20e and 20f

Kepler 20e and Kepler 20f were the first Earth-sized, rocky planets to be discovered orbiting a sunlike star. The planets are, however, too close to the star Kepler 20 for any liquid water to exist on them. This system also includes three other planets that are larger than the Earth.

NUMBER OF PLANETS 5

CONSTELLATION Lyra

DISTANCE 1,000 light-years

HD 10180's planets

As many as nine planets could be revolving around the star HD 10180, forming the largest known exoplanetary system. The two planets nearest to the star are similar in mass to the Earth. However, they are very close to HD 10180, which probably makes them too hot to support life. This artist's impression shows the first four planets in orbit around HD 10180—the first three look like dots near the star, while the fourth planet HD 10180d can be seen at the top.

NUMBER OF PLANETS	Up to 9
CONSTELLATION	Hydrus
DISTANCE	122 light-years

Artist's impression of planet
Kepler 20e near Kepler 20

Nebulae

Gigantic clouds of gas and dust called nebulae float inside galaxies. Some are dark clouds where new stars are born, while others are created by stars dying. Bright nebulae either reflect light from nearby stars or emit their own glow.

FOCUS ON...
TYPES
Nebulae can form in a variety of ways, each giving rise to a different type of nebula.

Carina Nebula
Star-forming region

The Carina Nebula is one of the brightest nebulae. Dust and gas in the Carina Nebula are lit up by many massive stars. The gas clouds in between these stars are moving at high speeds. This violent activity in the nebula produces high-energy X-ray radiation.

SIZE 300 light-years across
CONSTELLATION Carina
DISTANCE 8,000 light-years

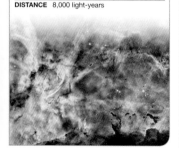

Lagoon Nebula
Star-forming region

This nebula is a stellar nursery in which many stars are being born. It is lit up by the energy of the hot, young stars. The Lagoon Nebula is so large and bright that it can be spotted with the naked eye in the night sky.

SIZE 110 light-years across
CONSTELLATION Sagittarius
DISTANCE 5,200 light-years

▲ Dense pockets of gas can become star-forming regions— such as the Trifid Nebula—which start to give birth to stars.

▲ Dying sunlike stars swell up in size and shed their outer layers, forming planetary nebulae, such as the Eskimo Nebula.

▲ Supernovae, such as Tycho's Supernova, produce an expanding shell of gas called a supernova remnant,

Eagle Nebula
Star-forming region

One of the best-known star-forming regions, the Eagle Nebula forms a glowing shape against the dark background of space. Many young stars have been found in this nebula, especially in and around the "pillars of creation"—gigantic, fingerlike columns of dust and gas.

SIZE	70 light-years across
CONSTELLATION	Serpens
DISTANCE	7,000 light-years

Cone Nebula
Star-forming region

Lying at the edge of an active star-forming region, this conical pillar of dust and gas is 7 light-years long. The Cone Nebula is bathed in light from infant stars in a neighboring star cluster known as the Christmas Tree cluster.

SIZE 7 light-years long, 2.5 light-years across at top

CONSTELLATION Monoceros

DISTANCE 2,700 light-years

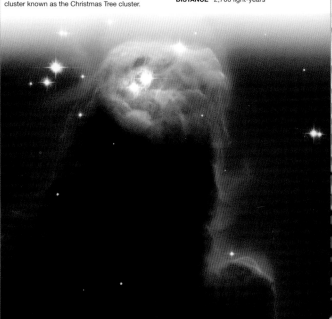

Orion Nebula
Star-forming region

The nearest star-forming region to Earth, the Orion Nebula appears as a faint, fuzzy patch of light, and is visible to the naked eye. It is heated by ultraviolet radiation from the Trapezium star cluster that lies within.

SIZE	30 light-years across
CONSTELLATION	Orion
DISTANCE	1,344 light-years

Horsehead Nebula
Star-forming region

Also known as Barnard 33, the unusually shaped Horsehead Nebula stands a full light-year above the surrounding clouds of hydrogen. This pillar of dust looks like the head of a horse or a knight on a chessboard. Hydrogen clouds behind it glow in the glare of ultraviolet radiation from the nearby star Sigma Orionis.

SIZE	16 light-years across
CONSTELLATION	Orion
DISTANCE	1,500 light-years

Ant Nebula
Planetary nebula

The Ant Nebula gets its name from its gigantic lobes of gas, which look a bit like the head and abdomen of an insect. A flat, doughnut-shaped ring of gas surrounds the lobes.

SIZE	1.5 light-years across
CONSTELLATION	Norma
DISTANCE	8,000 light-years

Helix Nebula
Planetary nebula

The closest planetary nebula to Earth, this looks like a giant eye in space. As with all planetary nebulae, the Helix formed when the star at its center shed its outer layers. Radiation from the remains of the star heats the dust and gas, causing the material to glow in bright colors.

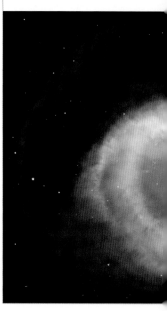

SIZE 2.5 light-years across

CONSTELLATION Aquarius

DISTANCE 650 light-years

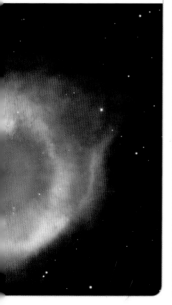

Cat's Eye Nebula
Planetary nebula

Scientists believe that the shining heart of the Cat's Eye Nebula may actually be a binary star system. Material given off by the central star at regular intervals formed the shells, or bubbles, surrounding it. Jets and knots of gas are scattered throughout this nebula.

SIZE 0.2 light-years across at core

CONSTELLATION Draco

DISTANCE 3,000 light-years

Cassiopeia A
Supernova remnant

Made of the remains of a supernova explosion, Cassiopeia A is a faint shell of expanding gas. It is expanding at a rate of 5 million mph (8 million kph). After the Sun, this is the next strongest source of radio waves in our sky.

SIZE	10 light-years across
CONSTELLATION	Cassiopeia
DISTANCE	11,000 light-years

Butterfly Nebula
Planetary nebula

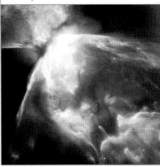

Crab Nebula
Supernova remnant

Created by a supernova that shone in the Earth's skies around 1045 CE, the Crab Nebula is still expanding at a rate of 3.4 million mph (5.4 million kph). Its vast clouds of hydrogen, sulfur, and oxygen are regularly rocked by shock waves from the star at the nebula's center. This star is a pulsar—a neutron star that spins very quickly and emits waves of radiation at regular intervals, like light flashing from a gigantic lighthouse in space.

SIZE	11 light-years across
CONSTELLATION	Taurus
DISTANCE	6,500 light-years

The Butterfly, or Bug, Nebula was created when the star at its heart turned into a red giant and shed its outer layers, shrinking into an incredibly hot white dwarf. Gas streamed out at high speeds, forming the nebula's winglike structures, which are still expanding.

SIZE	2 light-years across
CONSTELLATION	Scorpius
DISTANCE	4,000 light-years

Crescent Nebula
Planetary nebula

Dense packets of gas in this nebula form a semicircle, or crescent, around the central star, which will explode as a supernova in about 10,000 years. Radiation from the star causes hydrogen in the nebula to glow red.

SIZE	3 light-years across
CONSTELLATION	Cygnus
DISTANCE	4,700 light-years

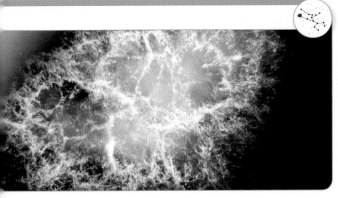

The surface of the star at the center of the Butterfly Nebula is at a searing temperature of

400,000°F
(222,000°C)

BUTTERFLY NEBULA
This planetary nebula is also known as the Bug Nebula or NGC 6302. The star at its center is blanketed by a colossal cloud of dust rich in the elements carbon and iron. The wings of the nebula are clouds of gas heated to more than 36,000°F (20,000°C).

Galaxies

Every galaxy is a large family of stars. The billions of stars that make up the Whirlpool Galaxy (left) seem to be laid out in colossal spiral arms that sweep through space. Other galaxies range from gigantic globes of ancient starlight to wheeling disks of clouds carrying thousands of infant stars.

MILKY WAY
Our own galaxy is spiral in shape, but it appears as a band of light across the sky. This is because Earth lies inside the plane of the galaxy so we see it edge-on.

What is a galaxy?

A galaxy is a collection of stars, gas, and dust held together by gravity. Galaxies vary in shape and size and also in the type of stars within them. Those with plenty of gas are rich in young blue-white stars, while galaxies lacking in gas are made only of older red and yellow stars.

Naming galaxies

From the 18th century onward, astronomers started discovering so many objects in space that most were not named, but were given simple catalog numbers. Some have familiar names, but many are still known only by these numbers. Major catalogs of deep space objects, such as stars, galaxies, and nebulae, include the Messier catalog with 110 objects and the New General Catalog (NGC) with 7,840 objects.

Messier 74 (M74) is a spiral galaxy

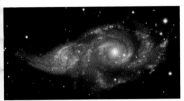

Colliding galaxies

Galaxies sometimes crash together in a spectacular pile-up, giving birth to thousands of hot stars. The collision causes a tug of war as each galaxy pulls at the other. NGC 2207 and IC 2163 form a pair of colliding galaxies that will merge in a billion years.

Supermassive black holes

At the center of every large galaxy is a supermassive black hole. This black hole can be more massive than a billion Suns. The gravity of the black hole pulls matter toward it, which forms a swirling disk. The supermassive black holes at the center of active galaxies fire out jets of particles and radiation.

TYPES OF GALAXY

Galaxies are classified according to their shape into five main types: spiral, barred spiral, elliptical, irregular, and lenticular.

A **spiral galaxy** is a giant disk with a ball-shaped nucleus, or center, and spiral arms.

The arms of a **barred spiral galaxy** extend from the ends of its stretched nucleus.

An **elliptical galaxy** can be shaped like a ball or an egg and has little gas or dust.

Irregular galaxies have no definite shape and are rich in gas and dust.

A **lenticular galaxy** is shaped like a lens. It has a central bulge but no spiral arms.

Galaxies

Galaxies formed from vast, spinning clouds of gas. Scientists think there are hundreds of billions of galaxies scattered across the universe. The farthest ones lie at the edge of the visible universe. The most common galaxies are faint dwarf elliptical galaxies, but we more often see the far brighter spirals and giant ellipticals.

Andromeda
Spiral

A family of 400 billion stars, the Andromeda Galaxy is the biggest member of the Local Group of galaxies—the Milky Way's neighborhood in space. It is the most distant object that can be seen with the naked eye in the night sky and appears as a pale oval with a starlike point of light marking its brilliant center.

SIZE 250,000 light-years across

CONSTELLATION Andromeda

DISTANCE 2.6 million light-years

Triangulum
Spiral

The Triangulum Galaxy is also a part of the Local Group. It is smaller than both Andromeda and the Milky Way and has far fewer stars. However, stars are being born in it at a far higher rate than in the other two. This false color image of the Triangulum Galaxy shows ultraviolet radiation from many young stars.

SIZE 50,000 light-years across

CONSTELLATION Triangulum

DISTANCE 2.7 million light-years

Whirlpool
Spiral

A bright spiral called the Whirlpool Galaxy, or M51, is the larger of a pair of galaxies. Its smaller neighbor may have passed through M51 in the past, triggering star formation in it.

SIZE 80,000 light-years across

CONSTELLATION Canes Venatici

DISTANCE 23 million light-years

Sombrero
Spiral

The bright center of the Sombrero Galaxy and the ring of dust surrounding it make this galaxy look like a sombrero, a wide-brimmed Mexican hat.

SIZE 50,000 light-years across

CONSTELLATION Virgo

DISTANCE 28 million light-years

Messier 83
Barred spiral

With the disk of the galaxy facing Earth, Messier 83, or M83, looks like a giant pinwheel in space. Dark lanes of dust line its spiral arms and are clearly visible. The arms contain many star-forming regions, rich in young stars. These regions appear as reddish specks in images of the galaxy.

SIZE	55,500 light-years across
CONSTELLATION	Hydra
DISTANCE	14.7 million light-years

NGC 7479
Barred spiral

Astronomer William Herschel discovered this barred spiral galaxy in 1784. NGC 7479 has a distinctive long central bar made of dust and gas and its tightly wound arms make it look like an inverted "S" in space. The arms spin slowly and one of the arms appears brighter than the other.

NGC 7479 is a Seyfert galaxy—an active galaxy with an unusually bright, compact center.

SIZE	150,000 light-years across
CONSTELLATION	Pegasus
DISTANCE	105 million light-years

NGC 1097
Barred spiral

Most galaxies have a black hole at the center. The one that lies at the heart of NGC 1097 is 100 million times the mass of the Sun. The stretched central region of this galaxy is eye-shaped and it makes NGC 1097 look like a giant eye floating in space.

SIZE	5,500 light-years across
CONSTELLATION	Fornax
DISTANCE	45 million light-years

NGC 4150
Elliptical

Visible-light images of this old galaxy have revealed strands of dust at its center, while ultraviolet images show clumps of young blue stars in the region. Scientists think that NGC 4150 collided with a smaller gas-rich galaxy about a billion years ago, which provided it with enough material to form new stars.

SIZE	About 30,000 light-years across
CONSTELLATION	Coma Berenices
DISTANCE	44 million light-years

Messier 105
Elliptical

ESO 325-G004
Elliptical

ESO 325-G004 is the largest galaxy in a galaxy cluster called Abell S0740. Giant ellipticals like this are often found at the centers of galaxy clusters. This galaxy acts like a giant lens in space—its gravity magnifies light from the more distant galaxies in the cluster, making them appear brighter when seen from Earth.

SIZE	200,000 light-years across
CONSTELLATION	Centaurus
DISTANCE	463 million light-years

The elliptical galaxy Messier 105, or M105, is part of the Virgo supercluster of galaxies. M105 was discovered in 1781 but was not included in the Messier catalog until 1947. It is moving away from the Milky Way at a speed of 467 miles (752 km) every second and, as with many galaxies, its center hides a massive black hole.

SIZE 55,000 light-years across

CONSTELLATION Leo

DISTANCE 38 million light-years

Messier 60
Elliptical

The black hole at the center of this galaxy is 4.5 billion times as massive as the Sun and one of the largest black holes ever found. False colors in this image show X-rays streaming out of the galaxy's hot center.

SIZE 120,000 light-years across

CONSTELLATION Virgo

DISTANCE 58 million light-years

Spindle
Lenticular

Most of the Spindle Galaxy is made up of old and middle-aged stars. Great lanes of dust surround its nucleus, or center, which bulges slightly on either side. A blue disk of bright young stars extends beyond the dust.

SIZE 60,000 light-years across

CONSTELLATION Draco

DISTANCE 45 million light-years

Cigar
Irregular

The edge of this galaxy can be seen from Earth as a stretched, cigarlike mass of gas and dust. Its deformed shape is due to the gravitational pull of the nearby Bode's Galaxy, which has triggered a burst of star formation in the Cigar Galaxy.

SIZE 40,000 light-years across

CONSTELLATION Ursa Major

DISTANCE 12 million light-years

Small Magellanic Cloud
Irregular

Some astronomers believe the Small Magellanic Cloud is made up of the remains of a small barred spiral galaxy, which was distorted by the Milky Way's gravity at some time in the past.

SIZE 7,000 light-years across
CONSTELLATION Tucana
DISTANCE 200,000 light-years

Large Magellanic Cloud
Irregular

The Small and Large Magellanic Clouds were named as clouds before astronomers knew they were galaxies. The Large Magellanic Cloud contains many star-forming nebulae, including the Tarantula Nebula—the most active star-forming region in the entire Local Group—which can be seen in this infrared image of the galaxy.

SIZE 30,000 light-years across
CONSTELLATION Dorado
DISTANCE 160,000 light-years

Tarantula Nebula

The rate of star birth in the center of the Cigar Galaxy is 10 times higher than in the entire Milky Way.

Death Star
Active

This is an active galaxy—a galaxy that emits jets of particles and radiation from the black hole at its center. Astronomers found the Death Star Galaxy was shooting a jet of gamma rays, X-rays, and radio waves at a smaller galaxy about 21,000 light-years away—this looked like a laser beam fired by a Death Star station in *Star Wars*. The jet appears blue in this false color image.

SIZE	20,000 light-years across
CONSTELLATION	Serpens
DISTANCE	1.35 billion light-years

NGC 1275
Active

Two huge lobes of gas stretching from the center of NGC 1275 emit large amounts of radio waves.

This giant elliptical galaxy lies at the heart of the Perseus galaxy cluster and is also called Perseus A. The massive black hole at its center heats up gas, and glowing threads of gas stretch out of this central region, extending for up to 20,000 light-years.

SIZE 70,000 light-years across
CONSTELLATION Perseus
DISTANCE 237 million light-years

Fried Egg
Active

The Fried Egg Galaxy is a Seyfert galaxy—an active galaxy with an unusually brilliant core. Its core has a black hole at its center and is about 3,000 light-years across. It is made up of a disk of hot gas and dust orbiting the black hole. This material falls into the black hole, triggering jets of radiation from it. The core is surrounded by a lumpy ring of hot young stars, which gives the galaxy a blue-white tint.

SIZE 36,000 light-years across
CONSTELLATION Pegasus
DISTANCE 72 million light-years

Antennae
Colliding

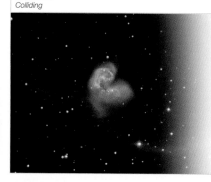

NGC 4038 and NGC 4039 are a pair of colliding galaxies called the Antennae Galaxies. They look like a pair of bright knots with two long strands of stars, like an insect's antennae, stretching in opposite directions. These are the spiral arms of the galaxies, which unwound after the galaxies collided.

SIZE	360,000 light-years across
CONSTELLATION	Corvus
DISTANCE	63 million light-years

The Mice
Colliding

The Mice, or NGC 4676, is the name given to two spiral galaxies that collided about 160 million years ago and are probably destined to merge. They have whitish bodies and long tails, which make them look a bit like mice. As with the Antennae Galaxies, the tails are the spiral arms that became unwound due to the collision.

SIZE	300,000 light-years across
CONSTELLATION	Coma Berenices
DISTANCE	300 million light-years

Cartwheel
Colliding

This galaxy was hit by a smaller one about 200 million years ago. This triggered shock waves that created an outer ring of young stars and a core that looks like a bull's-eye. The spokes of this "cartwheel" are ghostly spiral arms, which are forming slowly.

SIZE	150,000 light-years across
CONSTELLATION	Sculptor
DISTANCE	500 million light-years

HUBBLE ULTRA DEEP FIELD
The Hubble Space Telescope studied a tiny patch of the sky over 11 days to produce this composite image. It shows more than 10,000 galaxies, including some of the most distant ones, which formed shortly after the Big Bang.

To study the entire sky in the
same detail as this Ultra Deep
Field view would take Hubble

1 million
years
of uninterrupted work

Exploring space

Humans began to explore space in the second half of the 20th century, when scientists built powerful rockets—like the one shown here launching Space Shuttle *Atlantis*—which could transport spacecraft into Earth orbit and beyond. Today, dozens of countries take part in space programs through national and international space agencies. They use satellites and spacecraft to study Earth, the solar system, and the universe.

SPACEWALK
In 1984, astronaut Bruce McCandless II carried out a spacewalk outside Space Shuttle *Challenger* using a device that let him steer himself in space.

Types of spacecraft

A spacecraft is a vehicle that travels in space. Most spacecraft begin their journey at a launch site somewhere on Earth, and they are propelled into space by rockets. Spacecraft are made in many shapes and sizes, and carry different instruments depending on their missions.

Unmanned spacecraft

Robotic spacecraft have been exploring the solar system for about 50 years. These computer-controlled craft are packed with instruments and either fly past bodies in the solar system or orbit them (these crafts are known as orbiters). They send data and images back to Earth. This is an artist's impression of the Mars Express orbiter circling Mars in 2004.

Manned spacecraft

Astronauts started flying in spacecraft in the 1960s. Early manned spacecraft were small and had room for one astronaut who could fly for just a single day. Later craft could carry astronauts for many days—and even took them to the Moon. The *Apollo 16* spacecraft carried three astronauts on the fifth manned mission to the Moon in 1972. Seen here is its lander, or Lunar Module, on the Moon.

Landers and rovers

Orbiters may carry landers—craft that land on the surface of a planet or other body in space. In turn, landers may carry mobile vehicles called rovers, which can explore the body's surface.

Sojourner **rover explored Mars in 1997**

Space stations

Space stations are places in space where astronauts can live and work. Inside a station, such as the International Space Station (ISS), astronauts float about in weightlessness, while running experiments. The ISS was built from parts provided by five different space agencies, including the US's National Aeronautics and Space Administration (NASA).

ARTIFICIAL SATELLITES

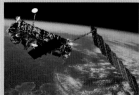

Envisat, an enviromental satellite

An object that orbits another is called a satellite. There are many natural satellites, or moons, in the solar system. Since 1957, humans have launched artificial satellites into orbits around Earth. Some are communication satellites while others study the environment or help people find their way around on Earth. Envisat—seen above—uses devices to study Earth's oceans and atmosphere.

Rockets

A rocket launches a payload, such as a satellite or spacecraft, into space. It is powered by a chemical mixture that burns to produce hot gases. These stream out of the rocket's nozzles, propelling the rocket upward.

FOCUS ON...
FUEL

Rockets use fuel to fly. A chemical called an oxidizer mixes with the fuel and provides oxygen to burn it.

Atlas V

A rocket is made up of two or more sections—known as stages—stacked on top of one another. Each stage has its own engines and fuel. As a rocket flies, one stage breaks off before the next one starts to burn fuel. Built in the US, Atlas V rockets use liquid kerosene as fuel for their first stage and liquid hydrogen for the second. Starting in 2002, these rockets have launched satellites about two dozen times.

SIZE 191¼ ft (58.3 m) tall

WEIGHT 737,400 lb (334,500 kg)

NUMBER OF STAGES 2

NUMBER OF LAUNCHES 30, August 2002–May 2012

Delta IV

Designed for the US Military, Delta IV rockets can carry single or multiple payloads in a single mission. There are five versions of this rocket, and each can be tailored to suit the payload. Delta IV rockets have been mainly used to launch military and navigation satellites.

SIZE 206–235 ft (63–72 m) tall

WEIGHT 550,000–1,616,800 lb (249,500–733,400 kg)

NUMBER OF STAGES 2

NUMBER OF LAUNCHES 19, November 2002–April 2012

▶ Solid-fuel rockets use a solid mixture of a fuel, such as aluminum powder, and an oxidizer, such as ammonium perchlorate. A spark ignites the mixture, which burns to produce hot gases. Solid-fuel rockets carry smaller payloads to low orbits. They also help liquid-fuel rockets reach higher orbits.

▶ Liquid-fuel rockets carry separate tanks for the fuel and the oxidizer. Liquid hydrogen fuel combines with liquid oxygen (the oxidizer) to produce water and heat. The heat turns the water into vapor, which jets out at high speed. Liquid-fuel rockets carry larger payloads to higher orbits.

Saturn V

Saturn V rockets are the tallest, heaviest, and most powerful rockets ever built. They were used in most of NASA's *Apollo* spacecraft missions, including *Apollo 11*—which saw the first manned landing on the Moon. A Saturn V rocket also launched Skylab—the first American space station—into an orbit around Earth.

SIZE	363 ft (111 m) tall
WEIGHT	6,699,000 lb (3,039,000 kg)
NUMBER OF STAGES	3
NUMBER OF LAUNCHES	13, November 1967–May 1973

Ariane 5

The Ariane 5 rocket is used by the European Space Agency (ESA) to launch spacecraft. In February 2011, the rocket launched *Johannes Kepler*—an unmanned spacecraft carrying supplies to the International Space Station (ISS). Weighing more than 44,000 lb (20,000 kg), it was the heaviest payload ever to be launched by an Ariane rocket.

SIZE	151–171 ft (46–52 m) tall
WEIGHT	1,713,000 lb (777,000 kg)
NUMBER OF STAGES	2
NUMBER OF LAUNCHES	62, June 1996–May 2012

Long March 3A

This Chinese rocket helps mainly with placing communication and navigation satellites into orbits around Earth. In 2007, a Long March 3A rocket launched *Chang'e 1*—the first Chinese spacecraft to orbit the Moon.

SIZE	172¼ ft (52.5 m) tall
WEIGHT	530,000 lb (241,000 kg)
NUMBER OF STAGES	3
NUMBER OF LAUNCHES	23, February 1994–March 2012

Soyuz-FG

Launched regularly from the Baikonur Cosmodrome in Kazakhstan, Soyuz-FG is the rocket used by the Russian Federal Space Agency to carry manned Soyuz-TMA spacecraft to the ISS. As well as ferrying supplies to the ISS, the rocket has also been used to launch satellites and unmanned spacecraft.

Proton

Although Proton rockets were designed to launch nuclear bombs for the Soviets, they were only ever used to carry craft into space. These rockets have been flying since 1965 and have been used more than any other, making them the most successful type of rocket. A modern version of this rocket, called Proton-M, was still in use in 2012.

SIZE	174 ft (53 m) tall
WEIGHT	1,529,600 lb (693,815 kg) (for 3 stages)
NUMBER OF STAGES	3–4
NUMBER OF LAUNCHES	377, July 1965–May 2012

SIZE 162½ ft (49.5 m) tall

WEIGHT 672,000 lb (305,000 kg)

NUMBER OF STAGES 2–3

NUMBER OF LAUNCHES
36, May 2001–December 2011

Soyuz 2.1b

This rocket is a member
of the Soyuz 2 family.
It was first launched in
October 2006 to place
two Russian satellites
in orbit around Earth and
will eventually replace
all other Soyuz rockets.

SIZE 151¼ ft (46.1 m) tall

WEIGHT 672,000 lb
(305,000 kg)

NUMBER OF STAGES 3

NUMBER OF LAUNCHES
8, December 2006–
December 2011

Spacecraft

Today, spacecraft are helping us to study the solar system's bodies up close and some are already heading beyond it. Astronauts have traveled to the Moon on the *Apollo* spacecraft, and robotic craft have been sent to study all the solar system's main planets, some asteroids and comets, and even the Sun.

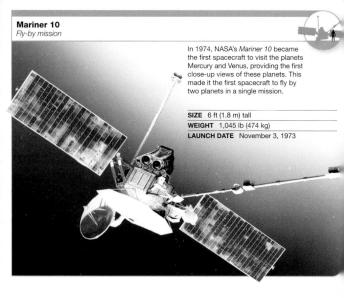

Mariner 10
Fly-by mission

In 1974, NASA's *Mariner 10* became the first spacecraft to visit the planets Mercury and Venus, providing the first close-up views of these planets. This made it the first spacecraft to fly by two planets in a single mission.

SIZE	6 ft (1.8 m) tall
WEIGHT	1,045 lb (474 kg)
LAUNCH DATE	November 3, 1973

Venus Express
Orbiter

Designed by the European Space Agency (ESA), this spacecraft has been studying the atmosphere of Venus since 2006. It is gathering data on why the planet's atmosphere rotates incredibly fast—the top layer of clouds spins around the planet 60 times faster than the planet's spin.

SIZE	4½ ft (1.4 m) tall
WEIGHT	1,540 lb (700 kg)
LAUNCH DATE	November 9, 2005

IKAROS
Space probe

In 2010, Japan launched a spacecraft called Interplanetary Kite-craft Accelerated by Radiation Of the Sun (IKAROS) to Venus. Its kite-shaped body works like a giant sail, catching the solar wind—the stream of particles blowing from the Sun—which creates a "pressure" driving the craft forward.

SIZE	66 ft (20 m) diagonally
WEIGHT	680 lb (310 kg)
LAUNCH DATE	May 21, 2010

Magellan
Orbiter

Magellan orbited Venus from 1990 to 1994 and mapped more than 99 percent of its surface in more detail than any earlier spacecraft. The mapping was done entirely using radar, which was able to penetrate Venus' thick atmosphere to image the ground below. The orbiter's equipment module and antenna are seen in this image.

SIZE	21 ft (6½ m) long
WEIGHT	2,280 lb (1,035 kg)
LAUNCH DATE	May 4, 1989

Luna 9
Lander

The Soviet Union's *Luna 9* was the first spacecraft to make a successful landing on the Moon. Its ball-shaped lander opened its petal-shaped panels and sent back images of the Moon's surface. This mission proved that landers would not sink on the Moon's surface.

Antennae opened automatically after landing

SIZE 2 ft (58 cm) across when closed

WEIGHT 218 lb (99 kg)

LAUNCH DATE January 31, 1966

Luna 16
Lander

Part of the Soviet Luna program, *Luna 16* was the first robotic probe to land on the Moon and bring back a sample of the Moon's soil. It drilled to a depth of 1½ in (35 mm) and collected more than 3½ oz (100 g) of soil.

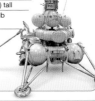

SIZE 10 ft (3.1 m) tall

WEIGHT 12,345 lb (5,600 kg)

LAUNCH DATE September 12, 1970

GRAIL
Orbiters

NASA's Gravity Recovery And Interior Laboratory (GRAIL) mission consists of twin spacecraft—Flow and Ebb, which are seen in this artist's impression in orbit around the Moon. These spacecraft study the Moon's gravity and internal structure. Each spacecraft is equipped with a MoonKAM (Moon Knowledge Acquired by Middle school students)—a special camera that takes pictures of the Moon's features as requested by school students. The spacecraft then send these images back to Earth.

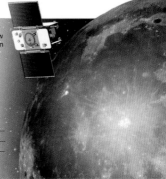

SIZE 3½ ft (1.09 m) tall (each)

WEIGHT 443 lb (201 kg)

LAUNCH DATE September 10, 2011

Lunar Reconnaissance Orbiter
Orbiter

The Lunar Reconnaissance Orbiter is currently orbiting the Moon. The main goals of this NASA spacecraft are to look for possible landing sites on the surface of the Moon for future manned missions and to take detailed images of the Moon's surface, creating a 3-D map with the data.

SIZE 9 ft (2.75 m) tall

WEIGHT 2,240 lb (1,018 kg)

LAUNCH DATE June 18, 2009

ARTEMIS
Orbiters

These two NASA spacecraft are currently in orbit around the Moon. They will eventually land on the Moon, where they will gather information about its surface and interior. The orbiters are expected to be sending data for several years.

SIZE 20 in (51 cm) tall

WEIGHT 280 lb (128 kg)

LAUNCH DATE February 17, 2007

Mariner 4
Space probe

NASA's *Mariner 4* was the first spacecraft to fly past Mars and transmit images of the Martian surface. It took 22 pictures, covering about 1 percent of the planet's surface, and also measured the density of the Martian atmosphere.

SIZE 9½ ft (2.9 m) tall

WEIGHT 575 lb (261 kg)

LAUNCH DATE
November 28, 1964

Mars Express
Orbiter

This was the European Space Agency's (ESA's) first mission to another planet. The spacecraft carried an orbiter and a lander called *Beagle 2*. The lander was declared lost when it did not send any signals after its expected landing. The orbiter, however, continues to study Mars.

SIZE 4½ ft (1.4 m) tall

WEIGHT 2,475 lb (1,123 kg)

LAUNCH DATE June 2, 2003

Artist's impression
of Mars Express
orbiting Mars

Viking
Lander

In 1971, the Soviet *Mars 3* probe became the first spacecraft to land on Mars. In 1975, the US launched the twin *Viking* spacecraft, both equipped with a lander and an orbiter. This was the first American mission to land a spacecraft on Mars. The landers tested the Martian soil and sent back some 3,000 photographs.

SIZE 7 ft (2.1 m) tall

WEIGHT 1,270 lb (576 kg)

LAUNCH DATE 20 August 1975

Device for
collecting
soil samples

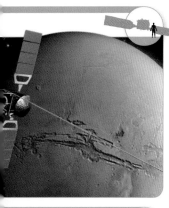

Mars Global Surveyor
Orbiter

The Mars Global Surveyor spacecraft was built by NASA and orbited Mars from 1996 to 2006—longer than any other spacecraft. It spent most of its time studying the planet's surface, where it discovered many long gorges that scientists believe were carved by running water in the past. Scientists know that liquid water existed on Mars millions of years ago when it was warmer. The planet has since become too cold for liquid water to exist on its surface.

SIZE	3¾ ft (1.17 m) tall
WEIGHT	2,270 lb (1,030 kg)
LAUNCH DATE	November 7, 1996

Artist's impression of Mars Global Surveyor orbiting Mars

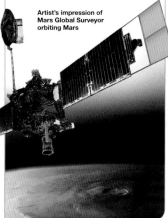

Mars Phoenix
Lander

NASA sent this lander to Mars to find traces of water on the planet. It landed in the planet's northern polar region and dug into soil in the area. It studied soil from below the surface and confirmed the presence of water-ice in it.

SIZE	7¼ ft (2.2 m) tall
WEIGHT	756 lb (343 kg)
LAUNCH DATE	August 4, 2007

Galileo
Orbiter

Galileo spent eight years orbiting Jupiter, between 1995 and 2003. It studied the gas giant's atmosphere and its largest moons. When approaching Jupiter, this NASA spacecraft released a small probe into the planet's atmosphere to collect more data.

SIZE	23 ft (7 m) tall
WEIGHT	5,650 lb (2,564 kg)
LAUNCH DATE	October 18, 1989

Hayabusa
Lander

Japan's *Hayabusa* became the first spacecraft to bring back a surface sample from an asteroid. *Hayabusa* visited the asteroid Itokawa and also studied its shape and structure.

SIZE	5¼ ft (1.6 m) tall
WEIGHT	838 lb (380 kg)
LAUNCH DATE	May 9, 2003

Voyager
Fly-by missions

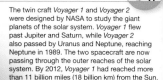

The twin craft *Voyager 1* and *Voyager 2* were designed by NASA to study the giant planets of the solar system. *Voyager 1* flew past Jupiter and Saturn, while *Voyager 2* also passed by Uranus and Neptune, reaching Neptune in 1989. The two spacecraft are now passing through the outer reaches of the solar system. By 2012, *Voyager 1* had reached more than 11 billion miles (18 billion km) from the Sun.

SIZE	18½ in (47 cm) tall (each)
WEIGHT	1,590 lb (722 kg)
LAUNCH DATE	*Voyager 1*: September 5, 1977; *Voyager 2*: August 20, 1977

Cassini–Huygens
Orbiter and lander

This artist's impression shows NASA's *Cassini-Huygens* spacecraft near Saturn's rings. *Huygens* was the name of the robotic probe that reached the surface of Titan, one of Saturn's moons. *Cassini*, the orbiter, continues to study Saturn, Titan, and Saturn's rings.

SIZE 22 ft (6.7 m) tall

WEIGHT 5,512 lb (2,500 kg)

LAUNCH DATE October 15, 1997

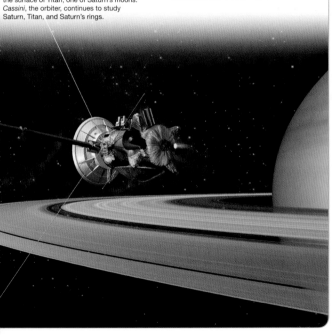

Gemini
Manned spacecraft

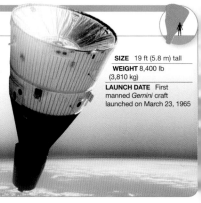

NASA's *Gemini* spacecraft gathered information about long-duration space flights, tested equipment, and prepared astronauts for the *Apollo* missions. NASA sent 10 manned *Gemini* craft into space. Each one could carry two astronauts and has three modules. The first module contained the astronauts, the second carried air and water supplies, and the third housed the engine to power the spacecraft. In 1965, *Gemini 7* spent a then-record time in space for a manned spacecraft, remaining in orbit around Earth for 14 days.

SIZE 19 ft (5.8 m) tall

WEIGHT 8,400 lb (3,810 kg)

LAUNCH DATE First manned *Gemini* craft launched on March 23, 1965

Apollo Command Module
Manned spacecraft

Each *Apollo* spacecraft was made up of modules. The cone-shaped Command Module carried astronauts to the Moon and back. After reaching the Moon's orbit, the Command Module would separate from the Lunar Module and one astronaut would continue to orbit the Moon in it.

SIZE 10½ ft (3.2 m) tall

WEIGHT 12,800 lb (5,810 kg)

LAUNCH DATE First launched on January 20, 1966 (test flight)

Apollo Lunar Module
Manned lander

The *Apollo* Lunar Module was designed to be lightweight so that it used less fuel. This was the lander section of the *Apollo* spacecraft. Each Lunar Module could carry two astronauts from Moon orbit to the lunar surface and back.

SIZE 18 ft (5.5 m) tall

WEIGHT 10,300 lb (4,700 kg)

LAUNCH DATE First launched on January 22, 1968 (test flight)

Columbia
Space Shuttle

Columbia is launched into space by rocket

NASA built five operational shuttles as part of its Space Transport Sytem (STS). The shuttle was the first spacecraft that could be reused. *Columbia* carried out the first orbital test flight of a manned shuttle. Astronauts John Young and Robert Crippen orbited Earth in *Columbia*, proving that the shuttles could be used to ferry astronauts to space and back.

SIZE	122 ft (37.2 m) long
WEIGHT	22 million lb (9.9 million kg)
LAUNCH DATE	First launched on April 12, 1981

SpaceShipOne
Manned spacecraft

SpaceShipOne was a reusable plane designed to fly into space beyond the atmosphere—at a height of about 60 miles (100 km)—and back. Its flight in June 2004 was the first manned space flight of a private spacecraft. It is part of a program that takes paying passengers into space as space tourists.

SIZE	28 ft (8.5 m) long
WEIGHT	7,940 lb (3,600 kg)
LAUNCH DATE	May 20, 2003

Lunar Roving Vehicle
Manned rover

The Lunar Modules of the last three missions to the Moon—*Apollo 15*, *16*, and *17*—each carried a Lunar Roving Vehicle (LRV). This was a battery-powered vehicle designed to drive over the Moon's surface. It could carry two astronauts, along with their life support systems and equipment. The LRV could move at a top speed of 11.5 mph (18.5 kph).

SIZE 10 ft (3 m) long

WEIGHT 465 lb (210 kg)

LAUNCH DATE First launched with *Apollo 15* on July 26, 1971

The farthest distance traveled by an LRV from its Lunar Module was 4.8 miles (7.6 km), during the *Apollo 17* mission.

Lunokhod 1
Unmanned rover

Lunokhod 1 was the first of the two unmanned Moon rovers built by the Soviet Union. The *Luna 17* spacecraft carried it to the Moon. Scientists controlled the rover via radio signals from Earth. It worked for almost 10 months, sent back more than 20,000 images, and analysed 25 soil samples on the Moon.

SIZE	4½ ft (1.35 m) tall
WEIGHT	1,665 lb (756 kg)
LAUNCH DATE	
November 10, 1970	

Curiosity
Unmanned rover

This artist's impression shows NASA's *Curiosity* rover on the surface of Mars. Its goal is to find out whether conditions on Mars can sustain life. The rover will also gather samples of rock and soil and study for signs of past life.

SIZE	10 ft (3 m) long
WEIGHT	1,985 lb (900 kg)
LAUNCH DATE	
November 26, 2011	

Camera for imaging surroundings

Opportunity
Unmanned rover

Two identical rovers, *Spirit* and *Opportunity*, were sent to Mars by NASA in 2003. Communication from *Spirit* ended in 2010 but *Opportunity* continues to examine the Martian soil for signs that water flowed there in the past.

SIZE	5¼ ft (1.6 m) long
WEIGHT	385 lb (174 kg)
LAUNCH DATE	July 7, 2003

A sojourner is someone who stays at different places—the rover was named after

Sojourner Truth,

a woman who traveled up and down North America to fight for equal rights for women in the 1800s

MARTIAN ROVER
This view of the Martian landscape was taken by the Mars *Pathfinder* lander. This spacecraft also carried a six-wheeled rover called *Sojourner*. The rover spent two months on Mars carrying out experiments to study the planet's atmosphere.

Manned missions

Humans traveled into space for the first time in the 1960s. The Soviet Union sent the first man into space in 1961, and just eight years later, the US landed the first astronauts on the Moon. Today, the only manned space flights are those to Earth orbits. A manned mission to Mars may be the next chapter in the story of human space flight.

Vostok 1

The first step in the history of human space flight was taken by Soviet astronaut Yuri Gagarin, when he orbited Earth in the *Vostok 1* spacecraft in 1961. After completing one orbit, *Vostok 1* headed back, ejecting Gagarin at about 4 miles (7 km) above the ground. He then parachuted to Earth.

DESTINATION	Orbit around Earth
DURATION	1 hour and 48 minutes
START AND END DATES	April 12, 1961
DISTANCE TRAVELED	25,400 miles (41,000 km)

Mercury-Atlas 6

Also called *Friendship 7*, *Mercury-Atlas 6* was the first American manned spacecraft to orbit Earth. About 60 million people watched a live television broadcast of its launch. Carrying astronaut John H. Glenn Jr., it flew to a height of 161 miles (260 km) before orbiting Earth three times.

DESTINATION	Orbit around Earth
DURATION	4 hours, 55 minutes, and 23 seconds
START AND END DATES	February 20, 1962
DISTANCE TRAVELED	75,679 miles (121,794 km)

Voskhod 2

Soviet astronauts Pavel I. Belyayev and Aleksey A. Leonov flew into space in *Voskhod 2*. While in orbit around Earth, Leonov became the first human to step outside his spacecraft and "walk" in space. Since then, astronauts have done many jobs involving spacewalks, such as constructing the International Space Station (ISS).

DESTINATION	Orbit around Earth
DURATION	1 day, 2 hours, and 2 minutes
START AND END DATES	March 18–19, 1965
DISTANCE TRAVELED More than 447,000 miles (720,000 km)	

Aleksey A. Leonov performing spacewalk

Apollo 7

This was NASA's first manned *Apollo* mission. Astronauts Donn F. Eisele, Walter M. Schirra Jr., and R. Walter Cunningham (seen here from left to right) completed 163 orbits around Earth while testing the life support, propulsion, and other systems on the spacecraft.

DESTINATION	Orbit around Earth
DURATION 10 days, 20 hours, 9 minutes, and 3 seconds	
START AND END DATES October 11–22, 1968	
DISTANCE TRAVELED 4,546,920 miles (7,317,555 km)	

Apollo 11

This mission was the first to land humans on the Moon. On July 20, 1969, the Lunar Module of the *Apollo 11* spacecraft, carrying astronauts Neil Armstrong and Buzz Aldrin, touched down in an area of the Moon known as the Sea of Tranquility. The astronauts spent about 2.5 hours on the Moon, collecting rock samples, taking photographs, and conducting experiments.

DESTINATION Moon

DURATION 8 days, 3 hours, 18 minutes, and 35 seconds

START AND END DATES July 16–24, 1969

DISTANCE TRAVELED 950,700 miles (1.53 million km)

Footprint on the Moon's surface

Polyakov's marathon misson

Russian astronaut Valeri Polyakov stayed aboard the space station *Mir* for about 437 days, setting a record for the longest single stretch of time spent in space by a human.

DESTINATION	Orbit around Earth
DURATION	437.7 days
START AND END DATES	January 8, 1994–March 22, 1995
DISTANCE TRAVELED	187 million miles (300 million km)

Polyakov looks out of a window on *Mir*

Space Shuttle's final flight

After 135 missions to space, spread over 30 years, the world's first reusable spacecraft, the Space Shuttle, was finally retired in 2011. Its final mission saw *Atlantis* deliver supplies and spare parts to the International Space Station (ISS). NASA plans to continue ferrying supplies on commercial spacecraft, such as the *Dragon* craft created by a company called SpaceX.

DESTINATION	ISS
DURATION	12 days, 18 hours, 28 minutes, and 50 seconds
START AND END DATES	July 8–21, 2011
DISTANCE TRAVELED	5 million miles (8.5 million km)

Space stations

Since the 1970s, a total of nine space stations have orbited Earth, each providing a base for crews of astronauts to live in space and conduct scientific experiments. The latest, and the largest, is the International Space Station (ISS).

Salyut 7

In the 1970s, the Soviet Union began launching the *Salyut* series of space stations. The first one in the series, *Salyut 1*, was the first space station to orbit Earth. The seventh and final station in the series, *Salyut 7*, was in orbit from 1982 to 1991. It tested the docking of large modules (self-contained parts of spacecraft). This helped scientists to develop technology that was useful in building *Mir*.

SIZE	52 ft (16 m) long
LAUNCH DATE	April 19, 1982

ALTITUDE OF ORBIT
295 miles (475 km)

Skylab 1

This was the first American space station and it orbited Earth from 1973 to 1979. Its goals were to study the Sun and prove that humans could live and work in space for long periods.

SIZE 86¼ ft (26.3 m) long

LAUNCH DATE
May 14, 1973

ALTITUDE OF ORBIT
270–272 miles
(434–37 km)

Mir

Mir orbited Earth between 1987 and 2000. The station was constructed over a period of 10 years by adding new parts to the original module. Once complete, *Mir* included seven modules that provided living and working spaces for three permanent crew members.

SIZE 62 ft (19 m) long

LAUNCH DATE
February 20, 1986

ALTITUDE OF ORBIT
242 miles (390 km)

International Space Station

Four times larger than *Mir*, the International Space Station (ISS) is the largest man-made object ever to orbit Earth. No other space station has been manned for as long as the ISS. Since December 2000, teams from 15 countries have come together to design and assemble the station, which is due to be completed in 2013.

SIZE 356 ft (108.5 m) long

LAUNCH DATE November 20, 1998

ALTITUDE OF ORBIT
205–255 miles
(330–410 km)

Astronauts have performed 161 spacewalks over more than 1,015 hours since the ISS began to be assembled.

The ISS makes 16 trips around
Earth in 24 hours, which means
that astronauts on the station see
16 sunrises
a day

FINAL SHUTTLE
Between 1998 and 2011, spacecraft have made 135 trips to the ISS to deliver supplies and equipment. These include 74 trips by Russian vehicles and 37 Space Shuttle missions. The Space Shuttle *Discovery* made its final trip to the ISS in 2011. It is seen here returning to Earth for the last time.

Timeline of space exploration

- **1926** American engineer Robert Goddard launches a 10-ft- (3-m-) tall rocket using liquid oxygen and gasoline. This is the first rocket to use liquid fuel.

- **1944** Germany develops the V-2 rocket as a weapon. Modern space rockets are developed from it.

- **1957** The Soviet Union launches *Sputnik 1*, the first artificial satellite. *Sputnik 2* is launched with a dog named Laika. Laika becomes the first animal to go into space.

- **1958** The US launches *Explorer 1*, its first satellite.

- **1959** The Soviets launch *Luna 2*, which crashes on the Moon, becoming the first man-made object to reach the lunar surface. *Luna 3* sends back the first photographs of the Moon's far side.

- **1961** Soviet astronaut Yuri Gagarin becomes the first man to go into space.

- **1963** Valentina Tereshkova becomes the first woman to fly into space, aboard the Soviet *Vostok 6* spacecraft.

- **1965** Soviet astronaut Alexei Leonov becomes the first man to perform a spacewalk.

- **1965** NASA's *Mariner 4* becomes the first spacecraft to fly by Mars.

- **1966** The Soviet Union's *Luna 9* becomes the first spacecraft to land successfully on the Moon.

- **1969** Neil Armstrong and Buzz Aldrin become the first humans to walk on the Moon.

- **1971** The Soviet Union launches *Salyut 1*, the first space station. NASA's spacecraft *Mariner 9* starts orbiting Mars and detects volcanoes and canyons on its surface.

- **1972** NASA launches its eleventh *Apollo* mission—*Apollo 17* becomes the last manned craft to reach the Moon.

Twelve humans set foot on the Moon between 1969 and 1972. Nobody has been back there since.

- **1973** NASA's *Pioneer 10* becomes the first spacecraft to travel beyond the Asteroid Belt and fly past Jupiter.

- **1975** The Soviet Union's *Venera 9* lands on the surface of Venus and sends back the first pictures of the planet's surface.

- **1977** NASA launches *Voyager 1* and *Voyager 2*. Over the next few years they send images and scientific data from Jupiter and Saturn. *Voyager 2* later becomes the first probe to fly past Uranus and Neptune.

- **1981** NASA launches the Space Shuttle *Columbia*, the first reusable spacecraft.

- **1986** Five spacecraft from the Soviet Union, Japan, and Europe are sent to the returning Halley's Comet. The spacecraft *Giotto* photographs its nucleus, a first for a comet.

- **1990** NASA launches the Hubble Space Telescope into Earth orbit using a Space Shuttle. A problem with its mirror is not fixed until 1993, when it finally starts capturing images of distant stars and galaxies.

- **1992** NASA's Cosmic Background Explorer (COBE) satellite produces a detailed map of microwave radiation left behind from the early universe.

- **1995** NASA's *Galileo* spacecraft becomes the first to orbit Jupiter. It studies the composition of the planet's atmosphere.

- **1998** The assembly of the International Space Station (ISS) begins with the launch of its first module.

- **2004** SpaceShipOne flies to a height of 60 miles (100 km)—the first space flight by a privately funded manned spacecraft.

- **2005** The *Huygens* probe of the *Cassini–Huygens* mission lands on Saturn's moon Titan. It is the first landing on another planet's moon.

- **2011** NASA's launches the Mars Science Laboratory craft.

- **2011** NASA's fleet of Space Shuttles is retired after the final flight of Space Shuttle *Atlantis*.

- **2012** The *Dragon* craft becomes the first commercial spacecraft to successfully fly to the ISS and back.

- **2014** ESA's Philae probe (from *Rosetta* craft) becomes the first to land on a comet.

- **2015** NASA's *New Horizon* is the first probe to fly by dwarf planet Pluto.

NASA's five Space Shuttles made 135 trips to space between 1981 and 2011.

Amazing facts

BRIGHTEST STARS IN THE SKY

Apparent magnitude describes how bright a star appears when seen from Earth. These values follow a scale in which greater magnitudes have lower values. A star's luminosity is the amount of energy it gives off and is equal to the number of times it is brighter than the Sun.

Name	Apparent magnitude	Distance (light-years)	Luminosity
Sun	−26.74	0.00016	1
Sirius A	−1.47	8.6	25
Canopus	−0.72	310	15,100
Alpha Centauri A and B	−0.27	4.37	1.5
Arcturus	−0.04	36.7	170
Vega	0.03	25	37
Capella Aa	0.9	42.2	78.5
Rigel	0.12	772	117,000
Procyon	0.34	11.46	6.9
Achernar	0.44	139	3,150

MILKY WAY FACTS

★ The Sun is one of about **200 billion stars** that make up the Milky Way.

★ The mass of the black hole known as Sagittarius A*, which lies at the center of the Milky Way, is **4.1 million times** that of the Sun.

★ The diameter of the Milky Way is **100,000 light-years**.

★ There are **180 globular clusters** in the Milky Way. Some galaxies have thousands of these clusters.

★ The age of the Milky Way is **13.2 billion years**. This was determined by measuring the age of the oldest known stars in the galaxy.

★ The thickness of the bulging disk of stars at the center of the Milky Way is **2,000 light-years**. The surrounding gas makes the central bulge at least 6,000 light-years thick.

DID YOU KNOW?

▶ The Sun, like all stars, does not rotate like a solid. Its equator takes 26 Earth days for one rotation, while the poles take 34 Earth days.

▶ The light from the surface of the Sun reaches Earth in 8.3 min, but that light started out from the center of the Sun about 30,000 years ago.

▶ The Sun travels around the Milky Way once every 200 million years, covering a distance of 100,000 light-years.

▶ The Moon is constantly moving away from Earth. The distance between the two increases by 1½ in (3.8 cm) every year.

▶ Sunlight reflected by the Moon takes 1.3 seconds to reach Earth.

▶ Distances to the planets are measured by bouncing radar signals off them and timing how long the signals take to return.

▶ Neutron stars are the fastest spinning objects in the universe. They can rotate 500 times in just one second.

▶ Highly active galaxies called quasars are the most distant known objects in the universe. Even the nearest one is millions of light-years away from Earth.

SPACE AGENCIES

♦ NASA
The US's National Aeronautics and Space Administration (NASA) was set up in July 1958. It is the only space agency to have launched missions to all the planets in the solar system.

♦ Russian Federal Space Agency
Also called Roscosmos, this is the government agency responsible for the Russian space science programs and research. It was established in 1992.

♦ ESA
The European Space Agency (ESA) is a multinational space organization set up in 1975, with its headquarters in Paris, France. Nineteen countries are members of ESA, including the UK, Germany, Spain, and Italy.

♦ JAXA
The Japan Aerospace Exploration Agency (JAXA) is Japan's national space agency. It was formed in 2003 and works on research and development of technology for satellites and interplanetary missions.

♦ China National Space Administration
Established in 1993, China's national space agency has a successful manned spaceflight program.

Glossary

Active galaxy A galaxy whose central black hole gives off jets of particles and radiation.

Artist's impression A drawing based on scientific information.

Asteroid A giant chunk of rock orbiting the Sun.

Astronaut A person who travels in a spacecraft.

Astronomer A person who studies astronomy.

Astronomy The study of objects in space, such as stars.

Atom The smallest unit of a chemical element.

Basin A large, shallow crater.

Big Bang The event that triggered the formation of the universe about 13.8 billion years ago.

Binary star A pair of stars bound by gravity and orbiting each other.

Black hole An incredibly dense object with gravity so strong that nothing—not even light—can escape it.

Celestial equator An imaginary line on the celestial sphere, directly above Earth's equator, which splits the sphere into two halves.

Celestial sphere An imaginary sphere around Earth on which lie the stars and other bodies in space.

Comet A ball of ice and dust that orbits the Sun.

Constellation One of 88 regions of the night sky used by astronomers for finding objects. Also, the star patterns these regions contain.

Crater A bowl-shaped hollow on the surface of a planet, moon, or other body. Craters form due to collisions with asteroids or meteoroids.

Dark energy A mysterious force that makes up 72 percent of the universe and is causing space to expand.

Dark matter Invisible matter that does not emit heat, light, or any visible radiation, but affects its surroundings because of its gravity.

Declination A measure of position on the celestial sphere that is comparable to latitude on Earth. It shows the distance of a celestial body north or south of the celestial equator.

Dwarf planet An almost round body that orbits the Sun but is too small to be considered a planet.

Ecliptic An imaginary line on the celestial sphere along which the Sun seems to move over the year.

Electromagnetic (EM) radiation Energy-carrying waves, such as light, heat, and X-rays, that are given off by stars and other bodies in space.

Electromagnetic spectrum The complete range of EM radiation, from waves with the shortest wavelengths—gamma rays—to the longest radio waves.

Element A substance that cannot be broken down into simpler ingredients.

Equator An imaginary line around the middle of Earth that lies at an equal distance from Earth's poles.

Exoplanet A planet outside the solar system.

False-color image An image in which the colors of an object are not as they would be seen by the human eye.

Gravity The force of attraction between two objects or bodies in space.

Interstellar matter Gas and dust that occupy the space between stars in a galaxy.

Lander A spacecraft or part of one designed to land on a planet, moon, or other body.

Latitude The distance of a point on Earth's surface from the equator.

Launch vehicle A craft, usually a rocket, that launches spacecraft and other payloads into space.

Lava Molten rock released through a volcano or vent on the surface of a planet, moon, or other body.

Light-year The distance traveled by light in one year, or about 5.9 trillion miles (9.46 trillion km).

Longitude A measure of the position east–west of a point on Earth's surface. Zero longitude is defined by an imaginary line running from pole to pole and passing through Greenwich, London, England.

Luminosity The total amount of energy emitted by a star in one second. It describes the energy output of a star.

Magnitude Brightness of an object in space, expressed on a scale of number. The lower the number, the brighter an object is. Apparent magnitude is a measure of brightness as seen from Earth and absolute magnitude is a measure of an object's luminosity.

Mare (plural, **maria**) A smooth plane of solidified lava on the Moon.

Matter Any substance that has mass and occupies space. There are four main states of matter—solid, liquid, gas, and plasma.

Meteor A meteoroid that burns up in Earth's atmosphere, appearing as a streak of light in the sky called a shooting star.

Meteorite A meteor that reaches Earth's surface.

Meteoroid A lump of rock, ice, or dust, from a comet or an asteroid, that orbits the Sun. It can range in size from a fraction of an inch to several yards.

Module An individual unit of a spacecraft.

Neutron star A dense star formed when the core of a high-mass star shrinks at the end of its life. The original star has a mass of up to three times that of the Sun.

Nucleus The central part of an atom that contains the protons and neutrons. It also refers to the solid, ice-rich body of a comet, or the core of a galaxy, within which stars are densely packed, usually around a black hole.

Orbit The path of a natural or artificial body in space around another, more massive object. Artificial satellites, moons, planets, and stars are all held in orbit by the gravity of a more massive body.

Orbiter A spacecraft designed to orbit a body in space.

Payload The cargo carried into space by a rocket. It may include supplies, spacecraft, or satellites.

Planet A spherical object, made of rock or gas, that orbits a star.

Plasma The fourth state of matter, which forms when gas gets hot enough for a number of its atoms to break apart.

Pulsar A rapidly rotating neutron star from which we receive pulses of radiation.

Quasar A distant active galaxy that releases huge amounts of energy.

Radar A method of detecting the position and motion of a distant object by using a narrow beam of radio waves, which are fired at the object and detected when they are reflected from it.

Red giant A star that has swollen up after its core has converted most of its hydrogen gas into helium.

Redshift Lengthening of the wavelength of light given off from an object as it moves away from an observer. The object appears redder to the observer.

Ridge A chain of mountains or hills.

Right ascension (RA) Imaginary lines running on the celestial sphere from the celestial north pole to the celestial south pole.

Rover A mobile vehicle carried by a lander, designed to explore the surface of a planet or moon.

Satellite An object that orbits a body larger than itself. The Moon is a natural satellite of Earth. Artificial satellites are man-made objects in Earth's orbit.

Shield volcano A broad volcano with shallow slopes.

Spacecraft A vehicle designed to travel into space.

Spacewalk An activity performed by astronauts outside a spacecraft when in space.

Space Shuttle One of a fleet of five reusable spacecraft built by NASA for manned space flights.

Tectonic plates Huge chunks of rock that make up the rigid outer layer of Earth's crust.

Variable star A star that varies in brightness over time.

Volcano The site of eruption of lava and hot gases from within a planet or other body.

White dwarf The end-stage of a star that has finished burning its fuel—hydrogen and helium—and given off its outer layers, which turn into a nebula.

Zodiac An imaginary band on the celestial sphere, on either side of the ecliptic, in which the Sun, the Moon, and the planets appear to move.

Index

15 Monocerotis 81
47 Tucanae 75

ABC

Abell galaxy cluster 11, 107
active galaxies 110–11, 149
Addams Crater 46–7
Aldrin, Buzz 140, 146
Altair 79
Andromeda Galaxy 102
Ant Nebula 92
Antarctic ice sheet 48
Antennae Galaxies 112
Apollo 7 139
Apollo 11 140
Apollo 16 118
Apollo spacecraft 118–19,
    124, 132, 134, 139, 140, 146
apparent magnitude 76, 148
Aquarius 18
Arecibo telescope 29
Ariane 5 rocket 121
Armstrong, Neil 140, 146
ARTEMIS orbiters 127
Asteroid Belt 5, 37, 66, 68
asteroids 5, 35, 36, 37, 68–9
astronauts 118–19, 138–45
astronomers 14–19, 23
Atacama Large Millimetre
    Array (ALMA) 28–9
Atlantis Space Shuttle 116,
    117, 141, 147
Atlas V rockets 120
atmosphere 38–9
atoms 8, 10
barred spiral galaxies 101, 104–5

basins 44, 57
Betelgeuse 78
Big Bang 8–9, 11
black dwarfs 77
black holes 77, 101, 148
blue stars 78, 84–5
Brahms Crater 44
Butterfly Nebula 94–7
Callisto 60
Caloris Basin 44
Canyon Diablo meteorite 73
canyons 51, 54–5
carbonaceous (C-type) asteroids
    68
Carina Nebula 74, 75, 88
Cartwheel Galaxy 113
Cassini-Huygens spacecraft
    131, 147
Cassiopeia A 94
Cat's Eye Nebula 93
celestial equator 14, 15, 17, 19
celestial sphere 14–15, 16–19
Ceres 66, 67
Chandra X-ray Observatory 30
China National Space
    Administration 149
Cigar Galaxy 108–9
colliding galaxies 101, 112–13
Columbia Space Shuttle
    133, 147
comets 5, 35, 36, 37, 70–1
Command Module 132
Cone Nebula 90
constellations 14–19
Copernicus Crater 57
cosmic microwave
    background radiation 8, 147
Crab Nebula 12–13, 94–5
craters 35, 44, 45, 46–7,
    48–9, 56, 57
Crescent Nebula 95
Curiosity rover 135

DEF

dark energy 10
dark matter 10, 11
Death Star Galaxy 110
declination 14, 15
Deimos 59
Delphinus 16
Delta IV rockets 120
deserts 49
Discovery Rupes 45
Discovery Space Shuttle 145
Dragon spacecraft 147
Dragon Storm 53
dwarf planets 5, 35, 37, 66–7
Eagle Nebula 89
Earth 4, 6, 14, 39, 48–9, 149
ecliptic 14, 15, 17, 19
Eistla Regio 46–7
electromagnetic radiation 12–13
electromagnetic spectrum 12–13
elliptical galaxies 101, 102,
    106–7, 110–11
Enceladus 62
energy 10
Envisat 119
equator 14
Eris 67
Eros 37, 68
Eskimo Nebula 89
ESO 325-G004 Galaxy 106–7
Europa 59
European Space Agency (ESA)
    121, 125, 147, 149
exoplanets 86–7
expansion of the universe 7,
    8, 10
exploration, space 116–45
fly-by missions 124, 130
Fomalhaut 79
Fried Egg Galaxy 111
fuel, rocket 120–1, 146

GHI

Gagarin, Yuri 138, 146
galaxies 4–11, 98–115
Galileo orbiter 69, 130, 147
gamma rays 13, 30
Ganymede 58–9
Gaspara 69
Gemini spacecraft 132
giant planets 36, 40–3
Glenn Jr., John H. 138
globular clusters 75, 82, 148
Goddard, Robert 146
GRAIL orbiters 126–7
Gran Telescopio Canarias 26
gravity 10, 11, 36, 75, 76, 82, 100
Great Dark Spot 53
Great Red Spot 52
ground-based telescopes 26–9
Halley's comet 70, 147
Haumea 66
Hayabusa lander 130
HD 10180's planets 87
Helix Nebula 18, 92–3
highlands 46–7
Himalayas 48
Hoba West meteorite 72
Horsehead Nebula 5, 91
Hubble Space Telescope
    31–3, 114, 147
Hyperion 63
Iapetus 64
ice sheets 48
Ida 69
IKAROS 125
infrared radiation 12
International Space Station
    119, 141, 143–5
interstellar clouds 5
Io 36, 60–1
irregular galaxies 101, 108–9
Ishtar Terra 46

JKL

Japan Aerospace Exploration
    Agency (JAXA) 149
Jewel Box 83
Jupiter 36, 37, 40, 41, 52,
    58–61, 71, 130, 147
Keck telescopes 26
Kepler 11's planets 86
Kepler 20e and 20f 86–7
Kleopatra 68
Kuiper Belt 5, 37, 66
Lagoon Nebula 18, 88
Laika 146
landers 118–19, 126, 128–32
Large Binocular telescope 27
Large Hadron Collider 11
Large Magellanic Cloud 109
lenticular galaxies 101, 108
Leo 16
Leonov, Alexei 139, 146
life 4
light, visible 13
light waves 12
light-years 6, 21, 148
liquid-fuel rockets 121, 146
Long March 3A rocket 122
luminosity 76, 148
Luna 9 lander 126, 146
Luna 16 lander 126
Lunar Module 118–19,132, 140
Lunar Reconnaissance Orbiter 127
Lunar Roving Vehicle 134
lunar seas 57
Lunokhod 1 rover 135

M

M-type asteroids 68
Maat Mons 45
McMath-Pierce telescope 28
McNaught comet 71

Magellan orbiter 125
manned missions 138–45
manned spacecraft 118–19,
    132–4, 138–45
Mare Tranquillitatis 57, 140
Mariner 4 128, 146
Mariner 10 124
Mars 5, 37, 39, 50–1, 54–5, 58–9
    exploration 128–9,135–7, 138,
    146, 147
Mars Express orbiter 118, 128–9
Mars Global Surveyor 129
Mars Phoenix lander 129
Mathilde 68
matter 10–11
Mead Crater 45
Mercury 38, 44–5, 124
Mercury-Atlas 6 138
Messier 60 Galaxy 107
Messier 74 Galaxy 100
Messier 83 Galaxy 104
Messier 105 Galaxy 106–7
Messier catalogue 100
meteorites 72–3
meteors 72
Mice Galaxy, The 112
Milky Way 6, 7, 17, 18, 20–1,
    78, 82, 99, 148
Mimas 61
Mir space station 141, 142
Mira 81
Miranda 64
Montes Apenninus 57
Moon 35, 56–7, 149
    exploration 126–7, 132, 134–5
    landings 138, 140, 146
    sides of 56
moons 5, 35, 36, 38, 40, 58–65,
    119
mountains 48, 57
multiple stars 78, 80
Mundrabilla meteorite 73

NO

Nakhla meteorite 73
NASA 119, 121, 124, 126–33, 135, 139, 141, 146–7, 149
NEAR Shoemaker spacecraft 68
nebulae 4, 5, 12–13, 74–5, 88–97
Neptune 36, 42–3, 53, 65
neutron stars 77, 149
New General Catalog (NGC) 100
Newtonian telescopes 24
NGC 602 star cluster 32–3
NGC 1097 Galaxy 105
NGC 1275 Galaxy 110–11
NGC 4150 Galaxy 106
NGC 7479 Galaxy 104–5
night sky 14–19
Nile River 49
North Pole 16
northern sky 16–17
nuclear fusion 76
Oberon 64
Olympus Mons 50
Oort Cloud 37, 70
open clusters 82–5
Opportunity rover 135
optical telescopes 24–5, 26–8, 30–1
orbiters 118, 125–31
Orion 15, 16
Orion Nebula 91

PQR

Phobos 58
Pisces 18
planetary features 44–55
planetary nebulae 77, 89, 92–7
planets 4, 5, 35–43
  dwarf 5, 35, 37, 66–7
  extrasolar 86–7
  giant 36, 40–3
  rocky 36, 37, 38–9

plasma 11
Pleiades 82, 84–5
Pluto 66–7
Polaris 15, 16, 80
Polyakov, Valeri 141
Proton rockets 122–3
Proxima Centauri 78
quasars 149
radiation 8, 9, 12–13, 30
radio telescopes 23, 25, 26, 28–9
radio waves 12, 25
red dwarfs 78
red giants 75, 77, 81
red supergiants 77
redshift 7
refractors 24
Regulus 78
Rhea 63
ridges 45
Rigel 80
right ascension (RA) 14, 15
rings 40–1
Rings of Saturn 41, 53
rivers 49
rockets 117, 120–3, 146
rocky planets 36, 37, 38–9
rovers 118, 134–7
Russian Federal Space Agency 149

S

Sagittarius 18
Sahara Desert 49
Salyut 7 space station 142
Sapas Mons 47
satellites, artificial 117, 119, 147
Saturn 36, 41, 53, 61–4, 130–1, 147
Saturn V rockets 121
Schmidt-Cassegrain telescopes 25
Scorpius 18
Sedna 37

Seven Sisters 84–5
Seyfert galaxies 104, 111
shield volcanoes 45, 47, 50
Shoemaker–Levy 9 comet 71
silicaceous (S-type) asteroids 68, 69
Sirius A 79
Skylab 1 space station 142
Small Magellanic Cloud 33, 109
Sojourner rover 118, 136–7
solar system 6–7, 34–73
  formation of 36
solid-fuel rockets 121
Sombrero Galaxy 103
South Pole 18
Southern Pinwheel Galaxy 4–5
Soviet Union 122–3, 138–9, 141, 142, 146–7
Soyuz 2.1b rocket 123
Soyuz-FG rocket 122–3
space
  exploring 116–47
  studying 22–33
space agencies 149
space probes 128, 147
Space Shuttle 116, 117, 133, 141, 145, 147
space stations 119, 141, 142–5, 146, 147
space telescopes 30–1, 30–3
spacecraft 117, 118–19, 124–47
SpaceShipOne 133, 147
spacewalks 117, 139, 143, 146
Spindle Galaxy 108
spiral galaxies 4, 99, 100, 101, 102–5
Spitzer Space Telescope 30
Sputnik 1 and 2 146
star clusters 32–3, 75, 82–5
star-forming regions 88–91
starhopping 15

stars 4, 8, 10, 14–19, 74–85, 100
  brightest 148
  colors 78
  life cycle 76–7
storms 52–3
Sun 4, 6, 14, 35–7, 149
supermassive black holes 101
supernova remnants 89, 94–5
supernovae 75, 77, 89

TU

Taurus 15, 16
Taurus-Littrow Valley 56
telescopes 22–33
Tereshkova, Valentina 146
Tethys 63
Titan 61, 147
Triangulum Galaxy 103
Trifid Nebula 89

Triton 65
Tycho's Supernova 89
Ultra Deep Field 114–15
ultraviolet rays 13
universe 4–5
  composition of 10–11
  formation of 8–9
  scale of 6–7
unmanned spacecraft 118, 124–31, 135–7
Uranus 36, 41, 42, 64
Ursa Major 15
US 120–1, 138–41, 146–7

VWXZ

V-2 rockets 146
V-type asteroids 68, 69
Valles Marineris 51, 54–5
valleys 56

variable stars 78, 81
Vega 80
Venus 38, 39, 45–7,1 24–5, 147
Venus Express 125
Very Large Array (VLA) 28
Very Large Telescope (VLT) 22, 23, 27
Vesta 69
Victoria Crater 51
Viking lander 128
visible light 13
volcanoes 45, 46–7, 50
Voskhod 2 139
Vostok 1 138
Voyager 1 and 2 130, 147
Whirlpool Galaxy 98, 99, 103
white dwarfs 77
X-ray telescopes 30
X-rays 12, 13, 30
Zodiac 18

Acknowledgments

Dorling Kindersley would like to thank: Lorrie Mack for proofreading; Helen Peters for indexing; and Claire Bowers, Fabian Harry, and Romaine Werblow for DK Picture Library assistance.

The publisher would like to thank the following for their kind permission to reproduce their photographs:

(Key: a-above; b-below/bottom; c-center; f-far; l-left; r-right; t-top)

1 NASA: Planetary Photo Journal Collection (c). 2–3 NASA: http://creativecommons.org/licenses/by/3.0 (c). 4–5 ESO: IDA/Danish 1.5 m/R. Gendler/S. Guisard/C. Thöne/http://creativecommons.org/licenses/by/3.0 (c). 5 Corbis: Ctein / Science Faction (br). NASA: European Space Agency (bl). 5 Corbis: Ctein / Science Faction (br). NASA: http://creativecommons.org/licenses/by/3.0 (tr). NASA: JPL (c). 6 NASA: Visible Earth / Reto Stockli / Alan Nelson / Fritz Hasler (c, tl); http://creativecommons.org/licenses/by/3.0 (c). 7 NASA: Spitzer Space Telescope Collection (cl). Science Photo Library: Mark Garlick (c). 8–9 The Art Agency: Barry Croucher (c). 9 ESO: Igor Chekalin/http://creativecommons.org/licenses/by/3.0 (c). 11 © CERN: Claudia Marcelloni / Max Brice (crb). © ESO: Nathan Benn (bl); Mark Weiss (clb); G. Brad Lewis / Science Faction (cb). NASA: Hubble Space Telescope Collection (tr). 12 Chandra X-Ray

Observatory: NASA / JPL-Caltech / Univ. Minn. / R.Gehrz (cr). NASA: Goddard Space Flight Center (c). 13 NASA: Compton Gamma Ray Observatory (c, tr); Goddard Space Flight Center (cr). NOAO / AURA / NSF: Jay Gallagher (U. Wisconsin) / N.A. Sharp / WIYN (tl). 20–21 Corbis: Dennis di Cicco. 22 ESO: Y. Beletsky/http://creativecommons.org/licenses/by/3.0 (bc). 23 ESO: http://creativecommons.org/licenses/by/3.0 (bc). 25 ESO: G. Hüdepohl/http://creativecommons.org/licenses/by/3.0 (tr). 26 Alamy Images: Tibor Agocs (br). 27 ESO: José Francisco Salgado/http://creativecommons.org/licenses/by/3.0 (b). NASA: (tr). 28 Corbis: Roger Ressmeyer (cla, br). 28–29 ESO: José Francisco Salgado/http://creativecommons.org/licenses/by/3.0 (b). 29 Corbis: Michele Falzone / JAI (br). 30 Chandra X-Ray Observatory: NASA / CXC / NGST (br). Getty Images: Purestock (bl). 31 NASA: Hubble Space Telescope Collection (bl). 32–33 NASA: Hubble Space Telescope Collection. 34–35 NASA: JPL. 35 NASA: Johnson Space Center Media Archive (bc). 36 NASA: Damian Peach (br). 37 NASA: (bl, br); Great Images in Nasa Collection (tr). 38 Corbis: Ocean (crb). NASA: Johns Hopkins University Applied Physics Laboratory / Carnegie Institution of Washington (clb). 39 NASA: Earth Day Image Gallery (tc); JPL / University of Arizona (tr); (tl, crb); Visible Earth / Reto Stockli / Alan Nelson / Fritz Hasler (clb). 40 NASA: Damian Peach (br). 41

NASA: JPL (br); (tl, tr). 42 NASA: JPL (bl). 43 NASA: Planetary Photo Journal Collection (cr). 44 NASA: Johns Hopkins University Applied Physics Laboratory / Carnegie Institution of Washington (c, tr, bl); Planetary Photojournal (br). 45 Corbis: Ocean (tr, cr). NASA: Johns Hopkins University Applied Physics Laboratory / Carnegie Institution of Washington (tc); Planetary Photo Journal Collection (cl, b, c). 46 Corbis: Ocean (tc). NASA: JPL (cr). 46–47 NASA: (tc); JPL (b). 47 Corbis: Ocean (tc, tr, c). NASA: JPL (br). 48 NASA: Planet Observer / Universal Images Group (cr). NASA: Visible Earth / Reto Stockli / Alan Nelson / Fritz Hasler (tc, tr); International Space Station Imagery (bl). 48–49 Getty Images: Stocktrek / Photodisc (bc). 49 NASA: Visible Earth / Reto Stockli / Alan Nelson / Fritz Hasler (tc, tr, c); Planetary Photo Journal Collection (br); Earth Observatory Collection (cr). 50 Corbis: NASA: JPL (tr). 51 NASA: JPL (tr, cr); Mars Collection (cr/Victoria Crater); JPL / USGS (br). 52 NASA: JPL (t); Damian Peach (tr). 53 NASA: JPL (t, cr); Planetary Photo Journal Collection (br); Solarsystem Collection (cb). 54–55 Corbis: Steven Hobbs / Stocktrek Images. 56 ESA/Hubble: J. Garvin/NASA/GSFC/http://creativecommons.org/licenses/by/3.0 (br). NASA: GSFC / Arizona State University (cl, bl, cr). 57 Getty Images: Stocktrek Images (b). NASA: GSFC / Arizona State University (tl, tc, tr, crb); Planetary Photo Journal Collection (cr). 58–59